SUPERNATION AT
PEACE AND WAR

SUPERNATION AT PEACE AND WAR

*Being Certain Observations, Depositions, Tes-
timonies, and Graffiti Gathered on a One-Man
Fact-and-Fantasy-Finding Tour of the Most
Powerful Nation in the World*

by DAN WAKEFIELD

An Atlantic Monthly Press Book

LITTLE, BROWN AND COMPANY · BOSTON · TORONTO

LIBRARY OF CONGRESS CATALOG CARD NO. 68-24098

FIRST EDITION

The author wishes to thank the *Atlantic,* in whose pages
part of this book was first published.

"Jungle War," by Richard Moore, © 1968 by Richard Moore,
appears in Appendix A by kind permission of the author.

ATLANTIC–LITTLE, BROWN BOOKS
ARE PUBLISHED BY
LITTLE, BROWN AND COMPANY
IN ASSOCIATION WITH
THE ATLANTIC MONTHLY PRESS

Published simultaneously in Canada
by Little, Brown & Company (Canada) Limited

PRINTED IN THE UNITED STATES OF AMERICA

To the Wisemans—Chippy, Fred, David and Eric, without whose help the author would rather not even imagine

Acknowledgments

THE author wishes to thank Emily Flint, Louise Desaulniers, Ellie Kane, and the whole third-floor back staff of the *Atlantic Monthly* magazine, who provided the most professional, expert, and sympathetic assistance in the editing of the manuscript and the survival of the author during the dire days approaching the deadline; Dolores Miele, who during the whole time of the travels so helpfully passed on the right communications and saved the ones that could better be borne at another time, and knew the difference; and finally, and without whom the above and the following would never have had a chance to happen, Robert Manning, who had the imagination and nerve and disregard for editorial fashion and safety to conceive of and commission the entire project and entrust it to a single individual. The writer so entrusted was not one whose by-line alone could ensure the box office success of the enterprise, which made the whole thing even more risky, uncommon, and challenging. The writer can now only hope that what follows does justice to the editor's own originality and faith.

Contents

Prologue

In which the author explains what he was doing, and what methods he used and did not use; why he encountered certain suspicions

I have just finished traveling for more than four months through a country that is fighting two wars, one at home in the streets of its cities, and the other 10,000 miles away in a tiny land whose people are of quite a different race and culture. The country through which I have traveled is regarded by most historians and experts as the most powerful nation of its planet and perhaps in the entire history of its planet. Many people regard this fact with satisfaction and awe, while others, even some within the supernation itself, find it a source of uneasiness, and even great fear. It of course is not for me to decide the proper attitude toward this great power, but simply to recount the findings of my journey and try to give you a sense of the life there during this crucial time in its history.

As with any great power involved in struggles at home and abroad, the situation is fluid, and by the time these papers will have reached you, there will have been certain changes, shifts of mood and emphasis and opinion, and yet it is doubtful that the basic life of the country will have drastically altered; doubtful for instance that either of its two great wars will have ended (although the domestic one subsides each year during the winter solstice, for it is fought on a seasonal basis) or that it will have lost its supremacy among the nations. There is also, of course, the remote and yet very real chance that the nation overnight could cease to exist, ironically because of the power it pioneered and possesses in the form of superbombs. In that unhappy event, this report will be of interest only as a kind of curiosity.

At the end of my travels, I have come to the nation's capital, and secured modest but comfortable lodgings, where I will stay while preparing this report, and occasionally venture out to speak with some of the leaders and attend some of the functions and ceremonies of the government. My rooms are at the top of a small third-floor apartment in the capital city, and the window affords me a pleasant view of a street that one could find in an ordinary section of nearly any city in the country. The great shrines of the nation are all within walking distance, and yet they are not visible from my window. The stately dome of its Capitol building, the stark needle monument to the "Father" of the country (reflected in a long, clear pool), and the great rotunda where sits the stone statue of the man who reunited the nation in a time of civil war, all are nearby but beyond my immediate vision. I see only trees and small neat houses of two or three stories, and a large red-brick church with stained-glass windows. It is difficult for me now, as it is for most of the citizens here, to realize that the nation is at war, with itself and its enemies halfway around the globe. From here, as from most of the country's windows, there are no signs or sounds of power or conflict or fear. At the end of the block, children are playing in a small park. Several of the neighborhood dogs erupt into sporadic barking, then subside. A busload of high school students goes by, cheering and chanting, on the way to an athletic event. The chimes of the red-brick church peal the solemn, melancholy notes of a hymn. You see, it is difficult here, as it is in most places throughout the country, to remember that any wars are going on, or that the nation is living through a time of its greatest power and perhaps its greatest trouble.

Most people do not sit around discussing the war or debating the best means to halt the decay of the inner city. They go to work, watch television, have a beer, take an aspirin, talk about football or sex or cards; they sleep, pray, love, and mourn.

I have tried to convey some sense of this common life that is lived by most of the people, most of whom see the wars and internal revolts and crises only in magazines and newspapers and on television screens. I have also tried to touch upon some of the mores, myths, and customs of the society as well as its more immediate concerns. In going about my researches, I adopted the garb, appearance, and manner of the predominant social and ethnic group of the nation, in order to be as unobtrusive as possible. In some areas, of course, this was a handicap, and the fact that I appeared as an ordinary white male of middle height, weight, and age, wearing a standard suit, shirt, and tie, aroused deep suspicions and sometimes hostilities, as I will recount. In a sense, however, these reactions seemed useful to my purposes of studying the prevailing customs and attitudes, and I feel that I gained more than I lost by sticking to the standard attire. In recent times it has become a popular approach for some researchers of this land and its people to adopt the appearance of whatever particular group was being investigated, in an effort to "pass" as one of the group. With my limited time and lack of technical assistance, however, it did not seem to me worth the extra effort to dye my skin black before entering a Negro ghetto, or to decorate myself with feathers, earrings, and luminous paints before descending into the circle of the subculture known as *hippi*e. I opted for the consistency offered by the more conventionally accepted costume.

I also attempted to be as straightforward as circumstances allowed in explaining to those natives I met and talked with that I was gathering materials for a report on their country, which also confused them. You must understand that in a supernation the gathering of information is usually carried on by vast networks and organizations; equipped with computers, recording machines, scientific questionnaires, and various other highly technical apparatus. Thus, I was often suspected either of being a secret emissary of one of those agencies or of being a poor misguided fellow who simply did not understand how things were done in a supernation. This attitude is not confined to academic circles, but is fairly prevalent throughout the whole society. While attending a dinner in one of the ghettos in a great city, a young member of the predominant local minority group asked me what I was doing, and when I told him, he said with obvious indignation, "You can't do that!" I asked him why I couldn't, and he said, "You need a research team for that."

Some writers nowadays travel in their own gaily colored buses or cars, but this again seemed too time-consuming for my mission, and so I went by commercial airlines, sipping my two-drink allowance and watching the aerovision movies just like all the other passengers.

Frankly, I was neither scientific enough nor colorful enough to have my mission seem acceptable or credible to many of the natives. Most of them, though, were kind enough to tolerate me and humor what seemed to some of them my mysterious enterprise. I am grateful to them, and to the hospitality that often was extended me. If this document should by chance fall into the hands of any of my hosts throughout this journey, I hope they will accept my real gratitude, and will not feel I have judged them or their country unfairly.

I

It is found that many of the natives are restless; assorted forms of revolt and protest are seen in the land

A. *In which a significant minority of the citizens of supernation do not like being in the war they are in when they learn they are in it; and what some of them do about it*

"And then came Vietnam. It sort of eased itself in and sat down next to me, like when you're at a party and suddenly realize that there's someone sitting next to you who you don't know and as you turn to look at him you realize that you're going to have to say something but you don't know what to say. What do you say, 'Hello, Reality?' But suddenly you realize that he's talking to someone else and you don't have to do anything. So you drift through the party hearing conversations, peoples' comments about the person; first you think he's a good-guy friend of the host; but others say he's a bastard, always comes to parties and makes a mess of things. Funny thing, you could go through the whole party and never even meet him, yet you could just happen to go to the bathroom and there he would be, and you know you would have to talk to him and that he will say something which will affect your whole life, might even get you killed, yet when you go to the bathroom you find he isn't there, and all you can hope for is that the host will soon bring the party to a close."

That is how the war came to Richard Lee, a junior at the University of Massachusetts at Boston, and that is how it

came to most Americans. Not only for those who oppose the
war but for those who support it and those who don't want
to think about it or don't know what to think about it, the
war "sort of eased itself in" to their consciousness. It even
seems to have come that way to the leaders of the nation who
are conducting the war, for they first said the nation could
not and should not fight it, and then they said if the nation
just fought a little bit it would soon be over, and then just a
little bit more and it would end, and the war kept growing
and the leaders kept seeing the end in sight. Many people
not only failed to see the end of the war but didn't even see
the beginning. There was no blare of trumpets to announce
it, no "day of infamy" to arouse the populace to the enemy
menace. The war that was not officially a war just kept getting bigger and bigger, and one day there were half a million
American troops in Vietnam and the nation was spending
$30 billion a year to fight the war, and yet even then it did
not seem as if a "real" war were going on to many of the citizens. Though economic and money problems loomed, the
economy of the richest nation in the world was booming, and the people were not subjected to the rationing of
goods and services and personal liberties that is usually
part of the circumstances of a "real war." Even those who
disapproved of the war were not forced to make a decision
about it one way or the other—unless they were of draft age
and therefore subject to serve and possibly to kill or be
killed in it.

---

i. *Some American boys choose exile over jail or Vietnam;
the Chinese set off a hydrogen bomb while I am eating in
a Chinese restaurant in Toronto with three exiles; more
are expected*

If a young man decides that he is unalterably opposed to serving in the war in Vietnam, he has what seems to be a variety of alternatives—indeed, it sometimes sounds as if he were in the position of a high school student browsing through college catalogues and trying to decide which campus is most to his liking. But after the various legal possibilities of deferment and dismissal are exhausted, he has only two choices. He can either go to federal prison for five years or go to Canada for the rest of his life.

Very few young men faced with the choice have gone to jail, even though many elder advisers on the draft consider that going to Canada is the more "radical" measure, partly on the grounds that at the end of the sentence the young man has the privilege of entering again the society that put him in jail. This of course is more often the view of those who are giving rather than receiving the advice. A number of young men in Canada said they were urged by religious and political counselors to choose jail before exile, and many of them gave it serious thought but finally felt something like Tom Zimmerman, who finally chose Canada instead. Zimmerman is a twenty-four-year-old graduate of the University of Kansas, with a B.A. in philosophy, and he said that before emigrating to Canada, "I really thought seriously about prison. I knew I wouldn't go to fight in Vietnam and I lost my student deferment when I went to graduate school. My draft board told me I already had one degree and they weren't going to defer me while I got another one, so I had to decide. I tried to think what would happen if I went to prison—what I would read there, and whether I would have a chance to teach classes in something for other prisoners. But I figured there was no way out, and that maybe it might ruin me by the time I got out. Some people say you're making a more effective protest if you go to jail, but I don't think many people even know you're doing it, and when you get out, you'd just be a criminal as far as most people in America feel."

In saying the choices are jail or Canada, I am speaking of Canada only as the most likely and popular place of exile. The exile could go to other places, including countries in Europe, but Canada is closest and most familiar in language and custom and landscape. While the United States has traditionally been known as a mecca for refugees fleeing other countries, Canada has quietly served as a haven for people fleeing the United States, particularly in time of war. Ever since the time of America's War of Independence (or, as it might be described today, its "war of national liberation"), Americans who didn't want to fight in the wars of their country have migrated north, but the current migration is the largest since the War of 1812, which has been described as the most unpopular war that the nation has fought until the present one.

The young men who go to Canada now are mostly college-educated and articulate young men, and they seem to represent a fair sampling of the sort of attitudes held by the anti-war students who are still in the United States. Mark Satin, a twenty-three-year-old American defector who was heading the main "antidraft" headquarters for American exiles in Toronto when I was there, was anxious to explain that "you'll probably be surprised by the guys who come here. People think they're mostly radicals or hippies or something, but most of them are really middle class."

The statement was uttered almost as a kind of defense or justification, for although Satin himself is more in the radical-hippie category, the classification serves as a kind of general condemnation in mainstream American society, a way of dismissing any person or group as not serious or responsible or significant. On the other hand, "middle class" is just as opprobrious a term to the radical-hippie segment, and so it was understandable that Satin added, "I mean middle class in the *best* sense."

Satin grew up in a small town in Minnesota and felt an instinctive sort of rebellion, but unlike Bob Dylan, he did not play the guitar and so had no way of expressing it. He finally found others of similar outlook when he got to college, and became head of the Students for a Democratic Society (SDS) chapter at a branch of the State University of New York. But he was generally bored, dropped out, and couldn't get into VISTA because he refused to sign a loyalty oath. He lost his student deferment but knew he wouldn't go fight in Vietnam.

"The war," he said, "made a lot of things clear to me. There were so many hypocrisies about it, and you got to see that your government was not the greatest and most honest in the world like you were brought up to believe."

He found his answer in a pamphlet called "Escape From Freedom," published by the Student Union for Peace Action, a Canadian student organization that began as a ban-the-bomb group. The SUPA "Anti-Draft Program" is now the principal organized agency for the relief and aid of American refugees from service in the United States "peacetime" army, and when he went to Toronto, Satin worked for a while at its headquarters there and was soon offered the job of "director" at twenty-five dollars a week.

His radical socio-political education seems to have been most furthered then, not by reading the massive array of pamphlets published by SUPA ("World Revolution and American Containment," "Let Us Shape the Future," and so on), but rather by a girl named Heather Dean, who did volunteer work around the office. Heather is a twenty-seven-year-old Canadian with long blond hair, thick glasses, and two children from a marriage that ended in divorce. In summer she is usually barefoot but sometimes wears white Courrèges boots.

Heather confessed that when Mark first came to Toronto he had short hair and wore baggy trousers. She corrected that, though, and now he wears tight-fitting pants and suede boots and is letting his hair get long. Heather is an intellectual, and reads the "Little Red Book of Mao" (*Quotations from Chairman Mao Tse-tung*), which seems to have become in both the United States and Canada the young radical's equivalent of Kahlil Gibran. Heather finds that you can turn to any page of it at random and find something applicable and useful to what's going on in your daily life. Later I got the book, and indeed, it had many inspirational passages, somewhat less poetic than Gibran but certainly as practical as Norman Vincent Peale:

> In time of difficulty we must not lose sight of our achievements, must see the bright future and must pluck up our courage.
>
> —*Quotations from Chairman Mao Tse-tung*

So much for the making of a radical, except to note that Mark Satin is a rather quiet, capable young guy who listens to people and questions things and does very well at his job of helping the exiles.

❖   ❖   ❖

**U.S. URGED TO SET
UP "PEACENIK" PRISONS**
Dallas (UPI)—If the U.S. declared war, it could set up concentration camps for people who are delaying the war, Rep. Joe Pool (D-Tex.) said yesterday.

> Pool said a declaration of war would
> bring "peaceniks" under sedition laws.
> Then, if they persisted in their action,
> the Justice Department could move
> them to concentration camps and leave
> them for the duration of the war.
>
> —*newspaper clipping on the bulletin
> board of the SUPA office in Toronto*

✦   ✦   ✦

One Saturday afternoon I sat around the front room of the
SUPA office, which is furnished in Sears, Roebuck contem-
porary and Salvation Army cast-off furniture, and decorated
with a large Canadian flag, some antiwar posters, maps of the
United States and Canada, a bulletin board with newspaper
clippings, and a wall area scotch-taped with old draft cards.
There is a desk and a typewriter where Mark Satin sits, and
a table with a hot plate, some cups, and a jar of instant
coffee. The room serves both as a lounge for the already
emigrated exiles and a reception room for newcomers seeking
advice and counsel. Many of the young men come up first to
look the place over before making their final decision. If they
cross over again as landed immigrants, they can apply for
Canadian citizenship after five years, but if they do this while
of draft age, they cannot return to the United States again
without being subject to arrest for both draft evasion
(penalty of five years' imprisonment) and "international
flight to avoid prosecution" (ten years' imprisonment plus a
$10,000 fine). At SUPA they can get information about the
best way to fill out their papers at the border, and which
border points have lately been reported as difficult or lenient
toward young Americans.

The first "customer" that afternoon was a guy with close-
cropped red hair who wore a checked sport shirt and khaki
pants and hardly seemed like a hippie. After he had talked

with Satin I introduced myself and asked if he had time to have a cup of coffee and talk about his coming to Canada. He hesitated a moment and then said he supposed he could. Outside he introduced me to two buddies who had driven up with him, and after telling them I was writing something, he laughed and said, "He's probably FBI," and the others laughed too, though not with real heartiness.

We went to a luncheonette down the street, and I asked Red's buddies if they were immigrating too. The one named Bob who wore a tweed sport coat said no, he had a I-Y classification ("qualified for military service only in the event of war or national emergency") and explained, "I got a letter from my psychiatrist." The other one named Phil, a tall guy with black-rimmed glasses, said he was going into the Peace Corps first and then he would have to decide after that.

Red came from New York City and had just got his B.A. in philosophy from a small liberal arts college in the Midwest, and he said he decided on Canada before he graduated.

"I had several alternatives in the States, like I could have taught in the New York City schools, they're very shorthanded and I was told I could get a deferment that way. But I feel sort of guilty about this whole thing. I'm not trying to be dramatic—I don't mean I stay awake nights or anything, but I feel guilty enough that I don't like the idea of staying in the country and serving it while it's carrying on this war."

He spoke deliberately, in a very even tone, and after just sipping his coffee for a moment he said, "Look, I'm not particularly politically oriented. I'd like to stress that. As far as I have any political philosophy at all, I guess it's anarchism. I'd call it apathetic anarchism. I think a lot of us feel it. Like the New Left guys at Berkeley who saw there was very little they could do to change the system and ended up in Haight-Ashbury."

Red's buddies seemed to agree with this conclusion. We talked through another cup of coffee, and then I thanked Red and promised I wouldn't use his real name because he was afraid it might make trouble for his father, who was a union official in New York. We got up to go and shook hands, and then Red paused and said, "One other thing. I don't want to sound like some martyr for a cause. I've tried to analyze the decision to come here as honestly as I can. But how much is selfish and how much is principle I really don't know. I know there are real moral principles involved, and yet I'm sure that selfish reasons enter in as well."

I thanked him for that, too.

Back at the SUPA office the next arrivals were a pair of big guys from New York in identical uniforms of sandals, levis, and sideburns. One had an M.A. in psychology but was about to lose his II-S deferment before getting the Ph.D., and so had decided on Canada. His main disappointment was that Yorkville, Toronto's imitation of Greenwich Village, seemed to be only teeny-boppers who were all up tight. After they left, a terrified-looking sociology student came in who stuffed his already bulging briefcase with literature on Canada, said he was also thinking about applying for C.O. status but wasn't too strong on religion, and departed mopping his brow with a handkerchief the size of a small tablecloth.

There were no newcomers for some time after that, and I introduced myself to a young man who had come in and started reading one of the papers on the couch. His name was John Pouttu, and he was twenty-six years old. He was short, wiry, and casually but neatly dressed in slacks and a crisp white shirt with the sleeves rolled up. He had a B.A. in literature, an M.A. in political science, and had won a National Science Foundation fellowship to pursue his studies for the Ph.D. at the University of Oregon. Shortly before entering the graduate program there, he was told by his draft board in the Midwest that he had "been in school long enough" and would be deferred no longer.

"I was really angry," John said. "I'd been studying and working for this all my life. I came from a poor family, I mean real poverty. We led an Appalachia-type existence though it was in the Midwest. When I was a child, we didn't have electricity. My father was trying to farm but he eventually had to give it up. Now he drives a truck. I found early that I could do well at school, and I liked it from the start. Ever since I can remember I wanted to be a college professor. Then when it was just in reach, the draft board said no, I had to go in the army."

He said it was not that alone that made him decide to leave the country, but also the Vietnam issue.

"I first became aware of Vietnam in 1961. I began to get active in the peace movement, and by '65 I was very active. As I switched from literature to studying politics, I became aware of the military power and authority in our own government. From a purely intellectual standpoint, in terms of political science, I think the war is lousy. It's cruel and hysterical politics based on a kind of last-ditch desperation. I might not feel so disgusted about it if I even felt it were in our own best national interest, but it's not. It's bad Machiavelli; I think it's destroying our own country as well as Vietnam." John introduced me to some friends in the office named Michael and Pat Rosenbaum, who were just about to go get something to eat, and John and I joined them. We walked a few blocks to a Chinese restaurant, and after carefully studying the menu, everyone ordered that renowned Oriental delicacy, the hot roast beef sandwich plate with veg. and pot.

The Rosenbaums seemed very young and collegiate, and in fact they had only recently been students. Mike had been at Rutgers, and after he and Patty got married they went to study for a year at the Hebrew University in Jerusalem, and had just returned and moved in with Mike's folks in New York City. That was only a temporary arrangement, but it turned out to be even more temporary than they expected.

"My parents," he said, "wanted me to stay out of the army because they were afraid I'd have to go to Vietnam. Well, when I took my physical I was told that because of a physical problem I wasn't qualified for combat, but I still could be drafted and serve as a noncombatant. My parents were delighted when they heard that, and wanted me to go ahead in the army. They didn't understand why I still didn't want to go in because of my opposition to the war in Vietnam. When I told my father I was going to Canada he kicked me out of the house, and called me a chicken and a Commie. If he thought I'd have had to fight in Vietnam he would have *sent* me to Canada. It's a tremendous kind of hypocrisy. What it comes down to is that he wants the war to be fought, but he wants other people's sons to fight it."

Mike hadn't found a job yet, and he wasn't really sure he had made the right decision in immigrating. He said one of his main consolations was that he thought a lot of his friends would be coming up too.

"Most of them are still in school," he said, "but I think a lot will come up when they're faced with the actual decision. I guess I wouldn't have made the sacrifice of giving up the States and coming up here if I didn't think my friends were coming too."

No one said anything, and our hot roast beef sandwiches came. There was an announcement from a radio at the cashier's desk that Red China had exploded a hydrogen bomb. No one said anything about that, either. The Chinese waiters were of course inscrutable.

"I don't know," Mike said, "maybe coming here wasn't the best thing after all."

John shrugged.

"We're here," he said.

◆   ◆   ◆

**GALLUP POLL
26% FAVOR
USING A-BOMB**

. . . Typical of the views of a "super-hawk" are those of a 54-year-old crane operator from Crescent, Ia.:
"We've got to push harder over there. We ought to bomb the daylights out of them and get the war over with. If the Army wants to use atom bombs, I say go ahead."

—*the Boston* Globe

◆   ◆   ◆

A couple were just leaving the SUPA office when we got back, and Mark said they had just come up from New York and the man would have no trouble getting a job because he was an experienced chef. The same pleasant prospects for employment—or anything else—did not seem to apply to a couple that came in about an hour later. He was eighteen and she was sixteen and both of them were scared. She was his girl and they weren't married and both of them were loaded down with wedding rings. When he got his induction notice and said he was going to Canada she said she was coming too, and they packed four suitcases and his guitar and drove from Miami to Savannah and took a plane the rest of the way. Mark got on the phone to see if he could find them a place to stay for a couple of nights with a Canadian family until they got settled. Some of the local families take people in like that.

Somebody asked the boy if he played the guitar, and he said yes and took it out of the case very gently, and after a little tuning began to play and sing a song about being on the road a long time and saying good-bye. The girl sat frozen still, listening and looking at the boy. He was tall and pale and there were no lines in his face. She had long, clean hair that caught the light and had no makeup on, and all those wedding rings.

Nobody knows how many young Americans come to Canada in order to avoid the draft, but it must be more than some of the estimates of Canadian officials who find it something of an embarrassment that these Americans are coming, since the United States government naturally doesn't like it very much. Most estimates have been "wildly inflated," according to Wilbur P. Chase, First Secretary in charge of consular affairs at the United States Embassy in Ottawa. Mr. Chase told a reporter that "I think you can count the number of genuine draft-dodgers arriving in a month on one hand." But I counted more than that in one afternoon at the SUPA office, and that was only in one of a number of Canadian cities where they come, and some don't come to SUPA at all because they don't like the left-wing political connotations, and so there must be quite a bit more than Mr. Chase thinks. The estimates of other observers outside the government ranged from around 3,000 to 10,000 in Canada overall, and most agreed that as draft calls rose and more graduate deferments were dropped in "nonessential" fields of study, more would be coming.

One of them wrote a poem, and it was published in the SUPA newsletter of June, 1967. The author uses the pseudonym of "Peter Milne." This is the poem:

> *Under each helmet the heart*
> *of a Lorne Greene, unelected*
> *Eisenhower to the Sixties.*
>
> *Our style has always been*
> *the sheepskin jacket, and*
> *our cars cannot yet outrun*
>
> *the stallion. The bad, small bets*
> *of our bored five-stud are backed*
> *with the magic of endless*
>
> *chips. The lives of cheaters*
> *cannot be pawned, for Texas*
> *is still a gun state. In the*
>
> *last hand myths are mortgaged as*
> *houses. Still our west will*
> *never be finally won.*
>
> *Oceans can't stop it. And*
> *the newsmen have all but*
> *forgotten the Indians.*

ii. *Antidraft tactics and resistance are practiced on the home front; some stay out by taking a "trip" to their induction center; I meet a runner, and also two "fine young men" who still won't go*

All over the country agencies and organizations have sprung up to advise young men on how to stay out of the army, and a group of clergy and lay leaders pledged to face arrest themselves for counseling youth to resist the draft.

One of the many groups in this movement is the Anti-Draft Union, composed primarily of students facing the draft, and often their female sympathizers. The Berkeley branch of the Union was holding a meeting one night on the campus, and I went over to see what was going on. The meeting was held at the Wesley Foundation (a collegiate Methodist organization) in a room that was mostly barren except for a soft-drink machine. The members were seated on metal folding chairs arranged roughly in an oval, and the chairman was reading the evening's agenda when I came in and took a seat. The first item of business was a report on the Union's activities in the "recruiting"—or as it might be termed in this case, "anti-recruiting"—of high school students.

A member assigned to report on the subject said that in the California area there was a great need for "converting high school students who are unsophisticated." He said one of the best programs of this kind was in New York City, where letters recently had been sent to all the senior male students of four different high schools inviting them to a meeting about resisting the draft, and 250 students turned out.

In Berkeley, the ADU's main work among high school students had consisted of talking to them about the draft during recess periods on school playgrounds, and passing out leaflets specifically addressed to high schoolers. The leaflet they had made up for this purpose had a cartoon of President Johnson wearing an Uncle Sam hat and crouching behind a line of students in caps and gowns who were walking out of a school building. The President held a graduation cap in one hand and a hand grenade in the other. The caption said, "Why shucks, I warn't very bright when I was their age, so I reckon they won't be verruh much smarter . . . yessir . . ."

A bearded fellow in the audience complained that the leaflet was bad psychologically, and in fact might alienate many high school students because it was too condescending. The first paragraph said:

HEY KID! Did you know that LBJ thinks you are stupid? During the hearings on the new draft law, it was reported that Johnson wanted nineteen-year-olds drafted first "because they would make less trouble." College kids would resent losing their privileges, it was feared, and might tell Johnson what they think of him. But the younger (and poorer) ones, who wouldn't be going to college, could be counted on not to offer much resistance. In other words, they're stupid.

The critic of the leaflet maintained that "if we all just remember back to when we were in high school, we know that one of the worst things someone could do was call you a 'kid.' That 'Hey Kid' would turn me off right away."

No one in the audience was so far removed from high school to have forgotten the truth of that, and most of them agreed that it sounded like a putdown.

It was decided to reword the leaflet for the high school students, and then another member was called on to discuss demonstrations and anti-recruitment activities at induction centers. The induction center expert said that he had some new ideas and techniques to discuss, but before going into them he said that "I would like for the man in the suit to give his name, and tell us what organization he represents, and why he is here."

I had been taking notes throughout the meeting, and I had just written down the last statement in my notebook when I looked up, glanced around the room at the forty or so young men and women present, and slowly, uncomfortably, realized that the sinister-sounding "man in the suit" was—

evidently—me. The others wore T-shirts or sport shirts and levis or khaki pants and sandals or boots or sneakers, and there simply wasn't anyone else who was wearing a suit. That was obvious. Everyone was staring at me.

I cleared my throat and revealed my name, the "organization" I represented, and my reason for being there. For a moment nobody said anything, and I realized what most of them were probably thinking, and it began to seem funny to me. I voluntarily added to my name, rank, serial-number identity the observation that the work I was doing was very difficult, because in places like this I was sometimes suspected of being an agent of the FBI or the CIA, while at other sorts of meetings I was sometimes suspected of being an agent of the Communist Party.

This brought some friendly and sympathetic laughter, and one guy grinned and said, "I move that we accept the man in the suit at face value."

This measure seemed to be adopted by unspoken general agreement, and I was greatly relieved. I was glad it didn't have to come to a vote.

The business of the meeting resumed, and the skeptical fellow told about some of his ideas for induction-center activities. He said that he and a few others had pretended to be inductees the week before, and so were able to talk to some of the real inductees inside the building and give them antidraft literature. He suggested someone try to get a blueprint of the induction center building, so that antidraft infiltrators would know where the exits and entrances and the toilets were, for purposes of getting in and out and hiding.

The members agreed that personal talks with the inductees were especially important since many of the guys didn't know there *were* any ways of getting out of the draft. If any of them seemed to be wavering about what to do, they could be advised even after they got inside to refuse to sign the question that asked about membership in subversive organizations, which usually delayed the whole thing for several months while their background was checked, and during that time a lawyer could be retained and other alternatives could be considered.

All these procedures seemed sound, but someone raised the question of the effectiveness of demonstrations and picketing outside the building. Some thought that this only made the inductees feel that the antidraft demonstrators were against *them,* rather than the war and the system. One guy said it depended on what kind of signs the picketers carried, and he had personally found that one of the most effective ones was the admonition to "Save Your Ass, Not LBJ's Face."

Another view was that regardless of the message, "Picket signs turn a lot of people off—especially conservative Americans who support the war. And believe it or not, there *is* such an animal."

There was general laughter, and a sense that not many people had ever encountered such an odd species.

A girl who agreed with the anti-sign sentiment added that "the way we dress alienates a lot of people too. I suggest we clean ourselves up before demonstrating."

There was hissing and groaning at this suggestion, but a possible compromise was offered. A student who had been at the University of Alabama the previous semester said in a deep drawl that "at Alabama we had part of our people demonstrating, and we also had our clean-cut-looking people mingling among the inductees and the onlookers."

"That's good!" said a bearded fellow who perhaps for a moment feared being shorn. "Have the hip people demonstrate and then have some reasonably-straight-looking people mingle with the crowd."

It was decided that this plan would at least be tested, and the business passed on to other matters, such as a report that the local fire marshal had come to the garage where a lot of the ADU literature was stored and taken out and burned a bunch of pamphlets called "Up Tight With the Draft"; a mimeograph machine was in need of repair; a site for a permanent office was discussed; and a party was announced for Saturday night.

✦ ✦ ✦

PUNISHMENT OF DRAFT FOES URGED BY SOME IN HOUSE

Washington, May 5—Members of the House Armed Services Committee demanded today that the Justice Department disregard the First Amendment right of free speech and prosecute those who urged young men to defy the draft law.

"Let's forget the First Amendment," Representative F. Edward Hebert, Jr., Democrat of Louisiana, told Assistant Attorney General Fred M. Vinson in a loud voice during hearings on the draft . . .

—the New York Times

✦ ✦ ✦

A representative of a more militant group was present at the meeting, and he handed out leaflets explaining the stand of his own organization, called the Resistance, which said that:

Those most active in the opposition to the war have deferments either because they are students or because of their unwanted politics. The RESISTANCE is a group of men who feel we can no longer accept our deferments so that others can go in our places. We REFUSE to co-operate with the draft and urge all other Americans to join us . . . we will openly violate

the selective service laws until the government is forced to deal
with our collective protest.

Those are the ones who burn their draft cards. The burn-
ings sometimes take place spontaneously, when a guy gets up
and asks somebody for a match and instead of his cigarette
he lights his draft card. It makes an orange glow, and lasts
for about five seconds. If there are other people present they
are hushed, as if watching a ritual. In a way, they are.

Some young men don't even bother. They don't want to
resist the system or accept the system, they just want to forget
the system and pretend it isn't even there. They go underground. It is easier now, with all the hippie communities
around where nobody has a last name anyway or is called
by something like Electric Buddha or Changes or Superjoe.
Those names are not on any records.

In Haight-Ashbury I met a young man called Don who
was tall and had blond hair falling down his forehead and
was reading his favorite author, who is Ayn Rand. He likes
her philosophy of antialtruism. He left home when he got his
induction notice, and he said he had traveled through forty
of the states of the Union, and he liked it best in Haight-
Ashbury but he doesn't know how long he'll stay. Nobody
knows where he is, least of all his family, and he figures he'll
just keep going. At the end of our conversation he smiled
and said, "Now you can say you've met a 'runner.' "

Nobody knows how many are running.

Some hippies, as well as many straight middle-class young
men, go to the trouble of trying to get a I-Y classification,
which means that "the registrant is qualified for military service only in time of war or national emergency," and that has
to be declared by the Congress, so Vietnam doesn't count. At
least it hadn't yet. The I-Y deferment is given "for physical,

mental, or moral reasons," which covers everything from homosexuality to kleptomania, with many other possibilities in between.

A favorite hippie technique for trying to qualify—or disqualify—for the I-Y is to get high before going to the draft board. LSD is preferred over marijuana because it puts you farther out and makes you seem less likely a prospect for marching along in step with a lot of other guys. But this technique doesn't always work, especially with draft boards where a lot of people have tried it. There was one guy who had some friends who worked it in Texas, and so this guy tried it at an induction center in the San Francisco Bay area. He got high on acid, and when he reported he was sent to the psychiatrist. The psychiatrist looked at him and said, "You're high, aren't you?" The guy said yes he sure was, and the psychiatrist signed something and then looked up at the fellow and said, "You'll like the army. It's a good trip." He was classified I-A.

✦ ✦ ✦

MILITARY institutional systems are horizontal and vertical hierarchies frozen for coordinating programmed corpses (soldiers) giving you the alternatives of either killing and burning people to death or going to jail for not obeying the established authorities—the general idols
            —*novas of diggers, Haight-Ashbury*

✦ ✦ ✦

The neighbors in the middle-class, Midwestern town where he was born and grew up and now lives with his family agree that Doug is a serious, responsible, intelligent young man. He is not a hippie or a rabble-rouser or the kind of kid who gets into trouble. He is thoughtful and independent but not a rebel. He respects his parents. They respect him. He won a scholarship to Michigan State University, and transferred to the University of Michigan at Ann Arbor in his sophomore year. Along with a group of other students from the university, he was arrested for participating in a sit-in at a local draft board, and served twelve days in jail.

One Sunday night I had dinner with Doug and his parents and another couple who are friends and neighbors. It was a Sunday night American meal of hamburgers cooked outdoors on the grill and french fries and cold beer. Before we ate I went down to the game room and talked with Doug about his experience.

"I wasn't a member of SDS, but I had a few friends in it, and I had gone to some meetings about the war," he said. "The actual decision to take part in the sit-in at the draft board was kind of sudden, it came kind of impulsively. But I had steeped myself in the literature about the war in Vietnam and I was very much opposed to it. I felt very powerless about it. I felt, you know, the Nuremberg kind of thing— that my country was involved in an unjust war, and I had a duty to oppose it."

Doug and the other participants in the sit-in were dragged away from the draft board by the police, and most of them had never experienced anything like it before.

"It was the first time in my life," Doug said, "that I was confronted with people who hated me—who didn't know me as an individual but who hated me. There was a crowd around when they took us out, and the people in it were red-faced and angry. Afterward, the university was kind of a sanctuary, but the people in the town were very upset about it. I began to feel isolated from people in the town, and I feared them.

"Right afterward I gave an interview to the press, about my

reasons for participating. Then I got what I guess were the usual number of crackpot calls, but to me they were frightening. They called me a 'Dirty Commie' and said, 'Go back to Russia,' and that kind of thing. My parents got phone calls too. There was one man who called up my father at two or three in the morning every morning for several weeks.

"Going to jail wasn't as bad as I was afraid it would be. I had a choice of serving ten days straight, or of keeping up my class schedule and serving twelve days on the weekends. [He had pleaded guilty to trespassing.] I didn't mind serving the time, but I was afraid about the other prisoners. I figured they would be townspeople and would be very hostile. But most of them didn't know why we were there, and the talk with them was mostly just gossip. When any of them asked what I was in for, I told them the truth. But when I explained it, they were more frightened of me than I was of them. The idea of a college student going to jail willingly was frightening to them."

Doug filed for C.O. status in his senior year and was turned down but is now appealing the decision. In the meantime he was called for induction and did not pass his physical, but he still is appealing for the C.O. because he wants to establish his position rather than just not have to go on the technical grounds.

Doug said he had filed for his C.O. status "on the basis of opposition to war in general, but I'm aware of the complexity of that. A lot of people talk about what would you have done in World War II, and I just don't know. I wasn't there, and it's philosophically impossible for me to say what I would have done then. All I know is that from my experience of my own lifetime there are no wars I would have fought in, and I can't foresee any in the next twenty-five years that I would want to fight in."

In another Midwestern city I was reminded of Doug when I talked to a high school senior who is president of his student council. Pat does not yet have to think of the immediate question of the draft because he will probably be accepted at a good university, but he is opposed to the war and worked in the Vietnam Summer project in his city. He said he didn't know exactly what he would do if he was drafted, but if it came to such a decision he would go and live in a foreign country, maybe England or someplace else in Europe, before he would fight in a war like Vietnam. Later his father told me that his son and his friends "think differently than my generation, they don't have the same feeling about the *nation* as such. I don't know whether it is better or worse, I just know it's different. I have many feelings against the war but maybe because of World War II, I feel we have to support the nation, that is our duty. These kids don't have that same kind of feeling, there are other things they feel are more important."

This lack of orthodox patriotism on the part of many young people worries their elders, and some of them have tried to think up ways of instilling the old unquestioning devotion to country in the children who will make up the next young generation. The American Legion has initiated a program designed for this purpose which it hopes to have adopted in elementary schools. The program consists of coloring a picture of an American flag with the red, white, and blue in the appropriate places, and learning the meaning of each of the different colors.

In his prophetic book *The Fire Next Time,* the American author James Baldwin said that there were certain wars in which Negro citizens would no longer fight, meaning wars against other colored peoples. If this has held true only for the very small minority of radical black power Negroes in the war in Vietnam, which requires killing Asian people, it has also less predictably turned out that there are evidently certain wars in which middle-class white Americans will no longer fight. This does not only mean those who have retreated to the near-total disaffection of the hippie world, but it also means boys who are otherwise considered "normal" or "average," ones who play tackle or are elected to student government. They are a small minority, but a significant one, and their numbers would seem likely to increase. The former president of the student body at Stanford University, David Harris, said that "if this country is going to police the world, it will have to imprison its youth."

Not all of them. But some of them. Ones like Doug and Pat.

---

iii. *A case of cultural overkill; how demonstrations happen but don't really count; a former Green Beret gives up marching*

When the President lashed out against the people who criticized the Vietnam War in "cocktail party conversations," he was striking at the very heart of the middle-class mobilization of protest. The cocktail party has long been one of the principal forums of dissent in the United States, and its use is not restricted to any one side of the political spectrum. History shows that left-wing groups in America used the cocktail party to rally support for the anti-Franco forces in the Spanish Civil War, and that the right wing employed the same tactic during the 1950's with its campaign called "Cocktails Against Communism." If Americans were restricted from forming committees and holding cocktail parties in behalf of political causes, it is doubtful that significant middle-class support could be mustered for any sort of protest movement.

As the protest against the Vietnam War policy escalated, so did the forms of entertainment employed to attract more people and contributions. In addition to a proliferation of cocktail parties, larger and more lavish events were launched, with rock music, psychedelic light shows, dancing, banjo trios, and comic piano players. There of course are some citizens who do not go in for that sort of thing, and these more serious types were offered lectures, debates, panel discussions, teach-ins, poetry readings, and rituals in which "Angry Artists" burned their own paintings in an ultimate act of defiance against the government.

What was possibly a new breakthrough in the entertainment-for-protest front occurred when some ingenious dissenters conceived the idea of a program that would mobilize both the rock 'n' roll units and the lecture troops in a single massive onslaught of antiwar sentiment. The event was sponsored by a group called the "Artists of Conscience" and staged at the Ambassador Theater in Washington, D.C., a former movie house converted to a hall for rock dances and psychedelic light shows (such conversion is effected by simply stripping the place of all the seats, leaving what amounts to a stage facing a large concrete cavity). The package program opened with the light show and rock dance, followed by speeches and readings by some of the literary artists who most vociferously oppose the war.

The middle-aged people mostly stood and watched during the first part of the program, in which all the senses were assaulted by that combination of flashing and flickering patterns of form and color accompanied by ear-blasting rhythms that constitute a "light show." The young people floated and swam serenely in the sound and light, and the middle-aged bore it in committed discomfort. One housewife who looked remarkably serene turned out to be wearing earplugs.

Much to the distress of the nonswingers, the intellectual performers were late, but just when it seemed that the light show would never go off, the vast hall was dimmed and the stage was lit in the old-fashioned, straight flood of white, and a master of ceremonies came to the microphone to introduce the literary stars.

After a poetry reading by Paul Goodman, the MC explained that one of the featured panelists had said that *he* wanted to be the MC, and that if the original MC didn't allow him to do so, "he said he would beat the shit out of me." This was a fitting introduction for Norman Mailer's performance of the evening. Mr. Mailer, who is, of course, the nation's most prominent example of the writer as public performer, was wearing a dark suit with vest and holding a cup that apparently contained something stronger than coffee. He scorned the microphone, saying that he would "do without electronics." Some people cheered his iconoclasm, while those in the back and in the balcony groaned because they couldn't hear very well. He told the audience, referring to the coming demonstration at the Pentagon, that "on Saturday we all goin' in and do something none of us done before."

He let out a deep, hoarse, braying sound, and then said, "The reason I have no respect for LBJ is he talks just like me."

He sipped from his cup, and said, "Reason I'm late is because I had to take a leak and there weren't any lights in the men's room up on the balcony here."

A lot of people laughed, but there were some loud "boos" from the back, and somebody called him "Bob Hope" and somebody else yelled "Boring!" but that did not at all deter

Mr. Mailer. Some of his colleagues tried to get him to sit down, but Mailer was firm in purpose, if swaying sometimes in body. He said he would call for a vote of those who wished him to remain and those who wished him to leave. There were loud responses for both proposals, and Mailer said, "In the absence of a definitive vote, the man who holds the power keeps it."

Finally he allowed Dwight Macdonald to come on. Macdonald explained that although he thinks Dean Rusk is an "idiot," that "Ho Chi Minh doesn't turn me on either." He mumbled a poem and rambled on about matters of which most of the audience had little interest, like the Boer War, and the "agricultural movement in the Philippines in the early part of the century." It got so it was hard to hear him above the buzz of the audience and finally, mercifully, he was done.

There was a standing ovation for the poet Robert Lowell, partly in recognition of his cultural heroism in having refused an invitation to the White House. Lowell was none too steady on his feet, and he came to the mike and said, "This is a zany evening, a queer occasion."

Lowell got through two poems and it seemed to be over, but Mailer came on again, and this time he seemed a little more sober. Perhaps recalling what he had said earlier, he now sought to make a kind of advance coverage of his behavior as it would later be reported. He said that the audience would see how the press distorts things when they read the papers the next day, and then he reached his finest moment of bravery. He said he knew there were reporters from the daily papers in the audience, and that they were chicken, and he challenged them to come up on the stage and confront him right then and there. No one went forward, and this showed how brave Mailer was, because there he was standing before an audience that largely regarded him as a hero, and he is a professional debater and amateur boxer and can yell louder than anyone and outcuss anyone, and yet not a single reporter wanted to walk up alone and engage in battle with him, a battle that would be of Mailer's own whimsical choosing before his own crowd. He stood there proudly, his stomach pushed out and his tousled hair thrown back and one hand thrust jauntily into his pocket, and one hand holding his mug. Fearless.

✦ ✦ ✦

> Reflecting the general frustration at the base [of Hill 875 near Dakto, Vietnam] at the slow and costly course of the fighting, one officer who had volunteered to fly into the perimeter in a helicopter said: "I don't care any more if I get back to the world, a world too stupid to stay out of the war, too stupid to know how to fight it, too stupid to know how to end it."
> —the Washington Post, November 22, 1967

✦ ✦ ✦

"This is America's chance to speak. Our names can save the lives of American soldiers and innocent Vietnamese. Our names can change history."
—NEGOTIATION Now!: A National Citizens Campaign for New Initiatives to End the War in Vietnam

Many people felt that just signing their names might not change history at all. Many had already signed their names, and had also done a lot of the other traditional things Americans do to effect a political change, like ringing doorbells and forming committees and writing their congressmen and voting for the candidate of their choice. Some were even disillusioned by the most sacred of American methods of effecting change, which is voting. In their last great national election for President one of the candidates said he believed that America ought to increase its military effort in Vietnam and win the war, while the other candidate assured the people he would not follow the dangerous policies advocated by his opponent and that he did not believe that American boys should be sent to do the job that Asian boys should do. The vast majority of Americans were greatly relieved when the man who urged an escalation of the war was defeated and the man who said no American boys should have to fight in it was elected.

As things turned out some people were disillusioned by all those traditional American means of changing things they didn't like, and so while many kept doing those things there were others that did things that weren't as traditional or acceptable. Some of them went out into the street and marched in demonstrations protesting the war, which for most middle-class Americans is a radical thing to do, and some of them did it for the first time. In the biggest of the marches a crowd estimated between 100,000 and 400,000 people from the Eastern half of the country went to New York City and 60,000 from the Western half went to San Francisco to participate in a "spring mobilization for peace" march. They were all different kinds of people from all different parts of the country, and they probably thought that would show a very strong and unusual sentiment against the war in all strata of the society.

Not necessarily. *Time* magazine, an invaluable publication for revealing what is socially and politically acceptable in the society at any given time, said that the main thing that the demonstrations showed was that "Americans in the springtime like to have fun."

Since at a minimum estimate well over 100,000 people

participated in the demonstration, there was no way to deny that it happened. But that was not the important thing.

The important thing was that it didn't count.

In America, there are several ways to prove that even though something happened it didn't count. The best ways are to show that it was mainly done by kooks or Communists, preferably both. Since there aren't enough Communists to make much of a turnout it is usually shown that the Communists were "behind" whatever the thing was, and since there are plenty of people whom others regard as kooks, it is usually shown that they were the main participants.

The *Time* magazine coverage of the demonstration was accompanied by seven photographs. The photographs showed (1) a crowd of youths gathered around a Russian flag and an upside-down American flag; (2) a pair of American Indians; (3) some long-haired boys burning draft cards; (4) Drs. King and Spock, the co-leaders of the march in New York; (5) a hippie with a tambourine around his neck; (6) a hippie girl with a banana around her neck; (7) a hippie girl with "Peace" painted under one eye. Under the three photos of the hippies was a caption which said, "Speaking eloquently for what the U.S. is trying to defend," leaving any literal-minded reader with the notion that the U.S. has a million troops stationed around the world in order to defend the rights of people everywhere to wear tambourines and bananas around their necks.

At any rate, one could obviously see by looking at the pictures that this was a bunch of kooks and possibly some Commies. (See picture of Russian flag.) The text of the story did not mention much other participation except for noting the presence of students from Smith and Vassar and some "Columbia University scholars," which hardly changed the overall picture for the average middle-class American reader.

This was the general picture of the event presented in most of the press, with varying degrees of intensity and emphasis. In a guest column on the editorial page of the New York *Times,* the "essayist and reporter" Marya Mannes lamented that among many other shortcomings, the march in New York did not, as it "ideally should have," represent a "cross-section of the American people." The only specific groups of people Miss Mannes mentioned in discussing the march were the "younger contingents" in their "best psychedelic regalia." Certainly there were a lot of kooks, if that is defined by hippie attire, and there were doubtless real-live members of the Communist Party. But they were hardly the majority or anywhere near it, and they hardly had "duped" more than 100,000 other Americans into being there.

As a prelude to my travels through the country I had gone to watch the march myself, and I stood on a street corner for more than two hours as it passed. During that time, which was less than half of the time of the march itself, I saw pass before me, many of them arranged in professional or geographic groupings, American veterans of different wars, wearing their veterans caps and some their medals; college professors wearing their academic robes (not just "scholars from Columbia" but from dozens of colleges and universities); students bearing banners of the names of their schools from the South and Midwest and East (not just Smith and Vassar); groups bearing signs identifying themselves as members of labor unions, of Negro organizations, Democratic clubs, women's organizations, and people from different towns and cities. There were housewives pushing baby carriages, men in business suits, older men with canes, a few on crutches, old ladies and children. There was a group with a sign that said, "Yellow Springs, Ohio, Says Stop the War"; a man smoking a pipe and holding a cardboard sign that was lettered in crayon: "Just Plain People Against the War"; a man wearing a veterans cap and carrying a sign that said, "Former Lt. in Korea Favors Negotiations." There were also the "colorful" hippies, bearing signs like "War Is a Down," and "War Is a Bad Trip." But except for the hippies and the "Columbia scholars," none of the above people appeared in the pictures or text of the *Time* coverage, or in Miss Mannes's lament about the nonrepresentative character of the march. No doubt many people in the march were rather discouraged when they got home and found that they had all been transformed into exotic long-haired hippies through the magic of modern journalism.

That's the way it was with most of the marches and demonstrations; they happened, sure, but they didn't count.

The only time that middle-class, "average" citizens were discovered to have constituted a large segment of one of the antiwar demonstrations was when a lot of them got beaten up. Most of them had never experienced that before, and being middle-class respectable citizens they held press conferences afterward and were interviewed in the papers and on radio and TV. That was in the demonstration in Los Angeles when some of the 20,000 demonstrators sat down outside the hotel where the President was having dinner, and the police rushed into the crowd swinging clubs and many people were badly beaten. Many of them were men like Dr. Mortimer Roth, a dentist from West Los Angeles, who went to the march with his wife and his eleven-year-old son and told what happened at a press conference:

"People around us came to a stop. It was impossible for us to move. I was at the south end of the hotel. I didn't hear the word to disperse. I didn't know anything until the police came at us. My wife was knocked down. My son was hit in the stomach with the end of a club. I tried to pick my wife

up, and a policeman said, 'Let her lie there! Keep going!' I
said, 'That's my wife!' and helped her up. I put my arm
around her and one around my son, and we moved away. As
we moved they hit me on the back with clubs six or eight
times."

People were shocked, not only because such a thing happened but because it happened to a respectable family man,
a professional man. Some people probably were even surprised that men like that took part in antiwar demonstrations. Maybe the only way for a dentist to be noticed in a
peace march is to get beaten up.

✦ ✦ ✦

HER BOOK COMFORTS FAMILIES

Mrs. William C. Westmoreland . . .
has put through dozens of calls this
week to the families of wounded servicemen.

In her little black book are such notes
as:

"Blue-eyed boy is scared but ok."

"Amputee is just waiting to go
home. His leg does not hurt but just
tingles."

"Boy who dies. Be sure to tell his
mother and daddy that the pain was
bearable and not to worry."

—*the Washington* Post *(Women's
Section)*

✦ ✦ ✦

Donald Duncan is one of the people who got disillusioned
with marching. First he got disillusioned with the military
kind of marching. He was a master sergeant in the Green
Berets and was decorated four times during his eighteen-
month tour of duty in Vietnam. At the end of it he turned
down a field commission of captain and instead returned to
the States and civilian life. He was working as a tree trimmer
around San Francisco, and one night he was at a friend's

house, and a guy came over who was active in the peace movement in the Bay area, and everyone got to talking about Vietnam. Duncan told how *he* felt about it after serving there a year and a half, and the peace movement guy asked him if he would say that in public.

Duncan said it in public for the first time at a peace rally in Oakland in 1965, and then he wrote it up in an article in *Ramparts* magazine with the arresting title: "The Whole Thing Was a Lie!"

In the article Duncan described the incidents that made him begin to question the war and said, "Little by little, as all these facts made their impact on me, I had to accept the fact that, Communist or not, the vast majority of the people were pro-Viet Cong and anti-Saigon. I had to accept also that the position 'We are in Vietnam because we are in sympathy with the aspirations and desires of the Vietnamese people' was a lie. If this was a lie, how many others were there?"

This was a shocker coming from a certified hero of the Green Berets, and yet it was still rather mild compared with the statements on the war from some of the retired generals and admirals who have spoken out against it, like former Marine Corps Commandant David M. Shoup, who said, "I believe that if we had and would keep our dirty, bloody, dollar-crooked fingers out of the business of these nations so full of depressed, exploited people, they will arrive at a solution of their own." Duncan didn't get into the realm of motives or causes, just the effects as he saw them in the countryside.

After his article came out, Duncan joined the editorial staff of *Ramparts,* and has continued to be active in the peace movement. But he is also disillusioned with *that* kind of marching. His first march was the one in Oakland in 1965 where he gave his first speech.

"I was impressed by how many middle-class people there

were in the march," he told me. "Lots of men in business suits, housewives with kids. But on TV all they showed were people with sandals and beards. Nothing that I or the other main speaker said was reported here.

"I don't think marches accomplish anything—except for the people in the march having a good feeling toward each other. It wouldn't matter if five million people marched. There'd just be a lot of heads broken."

I thought perhaps Duncan had changed his view when I saw him next as a speaker at the March on the Pentagon. But he said to the audience that the more everybody marched the bigger the war got, and that "we can march until we walk our way into the American version of the gas ovens."

He said the important thing now was resistance to the Selective Service System, which he felt exercised totalitarian control over the people. He referred to a Selective Service document called "Channeling," which says in its explanation of the overall aims of the draft:

> The club of induction has been used to drive out of areas considered to be less important to the areas of greater importance in which deferments were given, the individuals who did not or could not participate in activities which were considered essential to the defense of the nation. The Selective Service System anticipates further evolution in this area.

Duncan said that "if people stop registering, stop taking deferments, stop cooperating with the Selective Service System, it will fall apart." He said to the audience, "Don't go back to cooperating with the system when you leave here!"

Many people followed that advice, whether because of his own or others' urgings or not. Enough people followed it that a few months later the Attorney General announced the creation of "a special prosecuting unit to deal with the growing draft-obstruction movement in the United States." Soon after, Dr. Benjamin Spock, Yale chaplain William Sloane Coffin, and three other antidraft spokesmen were indicted for urging young men to resist the draft.

+ + +

Rep. James Haley (D.-Fla.) was loudly applauded when he proposed the following treatment for flag burners:

"I'd take them 200 miles out on the ocean, tie an anchor around their necks, throw them overboard and let them swim to any country whose flag they can respect."

—*the Boston Globe, June 21, 1967*

+ + +

B. *Large numbers of young people rebel against home, mother, country, school, and the affluent society which supports them anyway; subversion spreads to the hinterlands; collegians plan further guerrilla war on the colleges of their choice*

i. *An appeal is made for fresh fruit for the hippies; a taxpayer protests; prayer is proposed as an alternative to marijuana; Plastic Man substitutes love for nuclear vengeance*

The citizens of supernation have a passion for investigating, studying, and trying to understand themselves and their society. Gatherings such as the "conference" and the "panel discussion" on topics of concern have the status of ritual, and are believed to bring about changes in the problems so dealt with. Such events also provide social diversion for the mounting number of educated citizens who thirst for what they think of as intellectual stimulation, which is believed by many to provide "meaning" and "fulfillment" to human existence.

The National Forum, sponsored by the National Council of Churches, is one of the many groups and organizations engaged in such good works. The Forum is divided into local chapters called "Town Meetings," a term borrowed from the early history of the nation when most of its people still lived in towns and determined their local affairs at meetings.

"The Town Meeting of Southern California," tackling one of the most troubling issues of the land, sponsored a panel discussion called "Parents Meet the Hippies," which had a rather ominous ring of confrontation, reminiscent of certain old horror movies such as *Frankenstein Meets the Wolf Man.* A crowd of more than a hundred people, including a scattering of hippies but mostly composed of parents and curious elders, gathered at 8 P.M. one Sunday evening for the show.

Leonard Harris, the coordinator of the Southern California Town Meeting, announced that the moderator would be a lady who was responsible for arranging the whole panel, and who had been working long and hard to establish a bridge between adults and one of the local hippie groups known as the Diggers.

Lily Weiner is a hydro-psychotherapist, who Harris said is "known for her pioneering work" in that field, a science which evidently seeks to improve mental health by techniques involving the use of a swimming pool. Miss Weiner was a robust-looking lady of middle years, who explained that progress had been made in the effort to establish adult communication with the Diggers: "After a period of testing we have come to trust and respect one another." It was not the hippies alone that Miss Weiner was concerned about, but also their families, whose mental and physical states had seemed to have been laid waste by their rebellious offspring. "These youths who have flown the nest have left in their wake heart attacks, ulcers, and nervous breakdowns."

Retribution, however, was not mentioned and Miss Weiner stressed that "our goal is reconciliation," a condition that sounded more perilous for the parents than the youth after the damage that had already been inflicted.

Such problems are attacked in supernation by what is sometimes known as an "interdisciplinary approach," and thus the panel included not only representatives of the hippies but also experts from the fields of law, criminology, psychology, medicine, and religion.

The firm and yet tolerant attitude toward the problem maintained by the local police establishment was expressed by Lieutenant Onan Bomar, a Negro serving in the Community Relations Department of the sheriff's office.

"My appearance here," the Lieutenant was quick to explain, "doesn't mean that the sheriff's office supports the hippie community, but ours is not a blanket condemnation." He said his duty was to "serve mankind and to protect the peaceful against violence and disorder," regardless even of "dress or length of hair" as well as the more acceptable regardless of race-creed-and-color. Stressing again the police policy of equal prosecution of the law to all citizens, he noted that "though we don't approve of long hair and odd dress, that doesn't make such people criminals."

In spite of this enlightened attitude on the part of police, existing laws must be enforced, and the lieutenant warned that many of these kids are runaways, and older people who try to help them may be breaking the law. "Anyone who hides or abets a minor who is running away from home is guilty of a misdemeanor, for contributing to the delinquency of a minor."

This might have seemed technically to have made a criminal of another panelist, the Reverend Ross Greek, who is minister of the Hollywood Presbyterian Church. The Reverend Greek had opened his church to the summer influx of young hippies from all over the country, supplying them with food and allowing them to use one part of the church building as a "crash pad," which is hippie language for a temporary place to sleep. The Reverend explained that if the kids had run away from home, he tried to persuade them to call their parents, but did not notify parents without the child's permission. This practice seemed to adhere to more modern thinking, to which the letter of the law had not yet caught up. Anyway, his method was successful enough to have placed 143 girls, aged thirteen to seventeen, back at home in the past six months.

Lily Weiner praised the good works the Reverend was doing, and urged those in the audience to aid him in his ministry to the young. "Food is vital for Reverend Greek's work, especially fruit and vegetables. The church does feed them, as well as it can, but Reverend Greek is afraid they get too much starches."

Fortunately for the plight of these overstarched youths, the Hollywood Presbyterian Church was not the only agency contributing to their welfare. Also on the panel was Richard Pine, who was described as "the public relations man" for the hippie society known as the Diggers. The idea of the Diggers began in San Francisco, with some hippies banding together to help supply food and clothes for others, and several units sprang up in Los Angeles as well as many other hippie communities. One of the L.A. Diggers group was evidently having a hard time of it, and Mr. Pine came along and offered his services. He is not actually one of them, but at thirty-two feels he is able to serve as a go-between for them with the straight adult society, and he raises funds through lectures and appeals at public meetings and appearances before church and business groups. Pine said his Diggers in L.A. had helped house and feed about four thousand kids from all over the country.

"We know something's going on in this country. They come to us from Indiana, Montana, Nevada, all over."

A health problem that seemed more urgent than an unbalanced diet which also is besetting the young folks is the

spread of venereal disease. Dr. Walter Smart, chief of the
venereal disease division of the department of health in Los
Angeles, first made clear that "I don't want to convey the
idea that hippies are the only ones who have VD. We've had
epidemics of it here since 1957, and we can hardly blame the
hippies for what happened then."

The hippies had, however, brought a change in the type of
VD that was most prevalent in the area: "My own clinic in
the Hollywood Wilshire area mainly dealt with syphilis
among homosexuals. But due to the cooperation of the
homosexuals, syphilis is coming under control. Most of the
syphilis cases we have now are with people who have good
jobs, and have lived in the area for more than six months."

The new problem, coincidental with the influx of hippies,
is gonorrhea, which Dr. Smart said was up one third over last
year. "Most of these cases are young adults, fifteen to nineteen."

A special problem of the treatment of these youths again
seemed to indicate that the legal system was lagging behind
the social reality. According to law, twenty-one is the "age of
consent," and anyone younger must have parental consent to
be treated for a venereal disease, the doctor explained. Also,
they must live in or be residents of the county to be treated
by the public health clinic. Both these factors made it difficult to treat the hippies, since most of them were not legal
residents, most were under age, and many did not want to let
their parents know where they were, much less that they had
contracted a venereal disease and needed permission to have
it treated.

When these and other problems had been brought to light
by members of the panel, the floor was thrown open for
discussion, and it developed that many of the members of the
audience were not sympathetic to the burdens besetting the
hippies.

A small silver-haired lady with a cane seemed most anxious to express herself, and she rose somewhat shakily but then stated her question with clear and firm passion: "Do you think our overburdened taxpayers who have struggled and slaved for years to pay for our little homes should be saddled with thousands of dollars to pay for these freeloaders?"

Richard Pine retorted that "a lot more of your tax money is being used to kill people in Vietnam, and we want the money used here."

"We don't approve of Vietnam either!" the lady shouted, and received surprised applause from some of the audience. *"But,"* she continued, "we don't approve of freeloaders. I remember when they used to clean up skid row; if they made the drunks get out, the drunks would go home to their families and support them. They ought to do the same with you people."

"You tell 'em sister!"

This cry of approval came from directly behind me. It was uttered by a lady who had been muttering disapproval throughout most of the evening, and now her displeasure seemed to be growing. She was forty-five or so, and wore long magenta gloves, a green and purple blouse, and from each ear dangled a long chain with a red ball at the end, creating an effect that was not so much exotic as jarring. Someone on the panel started telling how the Diggers held free art classes that encouraged young talent, and the lady behind me shouted derisively, "Yeh, I know, I bet it's that surrealistic junk."

There were boos, and other people started talking at once, and Lily Weiner took the microphone and said, "Now, this is supposed to be like a real old-fashioned town meeting, and we must all respect one another's views."

The silver-haired taxpaying lady wanted to be heard again, and Richard Pine said that the hippies would like to prove to her they were her friends, and would like her to come to the platform and speak. There was a quick huddle among the discussion leaders, but the lady was already toddling to the platform, and it would have been difficult to push her back down, cane and all. She took the mike and said:

"I am Mrs. Schuyler. I am of course an American citizen, an honorable American citizen. I am a member of a group called Truth Forum Unlimited. We believe only the truth can make you free, and that there's a right and a wrong. All these young people come here bringing VD and drugs and bad habits. Their idea of love is promiscuous sexual madness!"

There were boos and jeers, and a lady stood up and said, "We don't have to listen to this!"

Lily Weiner, finding it hard to maintain the old-town-meeting atmosphere of mutual respect, shouted back, "Well, then you can *leave.*"

Mrs. Schuyler went on to say, "Last week a friend of mine was entertaining people, and hundreds of these hippies climbed over her fence, ruined her flower beds, and ate up all the food in the icebox."

There were cheers and applause. Lily told Mrs. Schuyler her time was up. The lady behind me said, "You can tell what nationality *she* is, the one running the meeting. She's a Jew—they want to keep control of everything."

Someone asked a question about drugs, and Herb Porter, a well-known lawyer in the area who has defended a number of young people in narcotics cases, explained very calmly that while LSD sometimes has very harmful psychological effects and all of its effects are not known or understood yet, marijuana is not harmful and is not addicting. The lady behind me jumped up and yelled, "That's not true, I saw a woman on television who said her daughter was in terrible trouble because of marijuana!"

"Try to control yourself," Lily advised her.

Porter went on to say that in fact with the rise of marijuana use in California there had been a decrease in the use of heroin.

The lady behind me rose again and shrieked, "Why do we need any of that? Marijuana or heroin or anything?"

A bearded young man came down the aisle, and with a taunting smile, handed the agitated lady a yellow rose. She threw it to the floor, scattering the petals, and the bearded guy turned to the audience with a smile like a lawyer who has proved his case and said, "Behold!"

"Why don't he *pray?*" the lady shouted, and stretching a magenta arm into the air, she exclaimed, "I have been *healed* by prayer, I can prove it!"

Nobody asked for proof, and someone asked Lily Weiner, "Do hippies use hydropsychotherapy?"

"No," she said, "but I wish I had a pool and could get them into the water with me."

There were a few other questions, and then Len Harris, the chairman of the Town Meeting of Southern California, said that their time was up for using the auditorium, but that he had found the discussion so stimulating that he hated to end it, and if anyone in the audience wished to continue they were welcome to come to his house. Mr. Harris's faith in the town-meeting system seemed to me to border on masochism, but he actually announced his address, and I took it down.

✦ ✦ ✦

HIPPIES HAVE A
QUIET HECKLER
Rep. Margaret Heckler (R.-Mass.)
told the League of Republican Women

yesterday that the bearded, rioting
hippie generation of today is searching
for "ideals," but has a tendency to
place individual decisions above legiti-
mate authority.

"It distresses me to see them this
way, for so many of them are really
fine people. They are just misguided,
they've forgotten the Constitution," she
said in a luncheon speech at the
Mayflower.

—the Washington Post

❖ ❖ ❖

After the meeting I got a ride over to Len Harris's house
with a fellow wearing a graying T-shirt who introduced himself as Plastic Man. I had seen him come forward down one
of the aisles during the meeting, asking to be heard, but no
one would ever recognize him. It turned out that he was the
leader of a rival Diggers group and felt that the panel was
hardly representative without his being on it.

I met Plastic Man's sidekick, a quiet fellow named George
who had recently left a theological seminary to try the hippie
life, and also a quiet girl with long hair and glasses who was
Plastic Man's wife (I never figured out whether I should call
her Plastic Woman or Mrs. Plastic Man, but she rarely said
anything so it wasn't a problem). The four of us drove over
in Plastic Man's car, and he explained to me how in being a
genuine Digger, he was just like a Mendicant in the Christian church of old, a person who was a beggar for alms but
gave the proceeds to others. I thought but did not say that
there were at least some superficial differences, as I had never
heard of a Mendicant who drove a new red Dodge Dart, but
then times change and there is no use splitting hairs. Plastic
Man was no doubt frustrated from having been "silenced,"
as he called it, at the general meeting, and so he was voluble
at the gathering at Harris's house. Mrs. Schuyler was
ensconced in a big armchair, and perhaps because she had

already had her say or was less comfortable speaking in small groups, she was fairly quiet.

A nice lady of forty or so named Libby asked Plastic Man how he started into the hippie life, and that set him off.

He explained that he is thirty-one, and that only six months ago he had a filling station and a small furniture business on the side, and was quite successful and middle class. What turned him on was blowing grass and reading Marshall McLuhan and Mao Tse-tung. Becoming more immersed in the new world opened up by that heady trilogy, he started letting his business go to hell, and by the time he got his income tax form he just scrawled across it "I Refuse to Co-Operate With a Corrupt Government," and sent it back.

Mrs. Schuyler wondered if she could do the same thing, and did he get away with it?

He said he did, but shortly after mailing in the IRS form he left the town and the business and just started drifting around and not using his old name anymore.

Libby, the nice red-haired lady, leaned forward on the couch and asked, "What did you say your name was?"

"Plastic Man."

"Ah," she said, nodding, "Plastic Man."

After that Libby and Mr. Harris and everyone else simply addressed him as "Plastic Man," just as they would call a person Henry or Hamilton or Jeremy or any other name that a person has.

Now the center of attention, Plastic Man began holding forth about how "Youth today" feel on different subjects, and a clean-cut young insurance underwriter asked him, "How can you speak for the youth of today when you've said you're thirty-one, and I'm twenty-four and I don't agree with you and I'm younger?"

"Ah, but you can be old at twenty-four," Plastic Man retorted.

The underwriter fired back that he knew a lot about this stuff too: when he was in Vietnam he learned to smoke pot along with his buddies, and what was such a big deal about that?

Plastic Man was very interested in the use of pot among the servicemen over there, and the underwriter assured him it was very common, and that you could buy it from the Montagnards very cheap; in Vietnamese money it was something like five or ten piasters for a stick. Everyone started to figure out how many piasters there were to a dollar, and it was agreed that this was a very good price.

I asked the underwriter how he felt now about the war in Vietnam, and he said, "It's funny. When I went over I was sort of buoyed up by the feeling that I was serving my country and all, and sort of a hero, but that was in '64. Just before I came home in '66, guys warned me I'd better expect to find that most people didn't support the war and would be against me. It was pretty much that way."

Plastic Man said all that was interesting, and that he was so much against the war that, "before I discovered Love, I mean the hippie ethic and all of it, I had a plan to put a small nuclear device in the Pentagon and blow the whole thing up. Now I see that's not the answer, but there may be some people who haven't learned about Love and might still do it."

Libby gasped at the idea, but the underwriter who was a veteran smiled, and said very politely, "You'll forgive me, Plastic Man, if I doubt your capacity to set off a small nuclear weapon."

Plastic Man only laughed.

After several hours this old-fashioned town meeting began to break up. When everyone was standing, Libby asked a quiet girl named Sharron what *she* did, and Sharron said she worked in the kitchen at the Hollywood Presbyterian

Church crash pad, and that's how she got the scars on her face. That sort of got everyone's attention, and Sharron explained that she had had a fight with another girl who was to prepare dinner, and the other girl was jealous and went for her eyes, but luckily she only got her fingernails in Sharron's cheeks, and the scars would probably eventually go away.

Libby said, "My God, I was really jealous of you people having all that Love, but I guess you're no different than the rest of us."

Nobody answered, and then Libby put on her coat and said, "You know, I really am disillusioned," and she said it with real sadness.

Many people felt the same way after getting a firsthand glimpse of the hippie scene.

✦ ✦ ✦

DIAL H FOR HELP

In a bleak room on the third floor of the Fulton County Health Department, Dr. Charles Edwards sat hunched over a telephone in a life-or-death conversation with an Atlanta businessman who was holed up in a posh suburban home, a loaded shotgun at his fingertips. He was one of at least twenty despairing and desperate Atlantans who each day call Fulton County's new Suicide Prevention Center. . . .

The center, a row of four bare offices equipped with telephones, is Atlanta's first attempt to deal with a social sickness which last year took the lives of an estimated 50,000 Americans and became the tenth-rank killer in the country. . . .

—Atlanta *Magazine*

✦ ✦ ✦

Libby isn't the only one who was disappointed. Despite all the hostility of the older generation there has been and in some degree still is an element of older people "rooting for" the hippies, hoping perhaps even in secret that the seemingly free young kids would find a better way than their elders, a release from all the hang-ups and hatred. The proper or straight society is for many of its members a dismal failure, and there are those within its well-shod, well-housed boundaries who feel too set in its patterns to escape but feel disheartened enough about its values and rewards to wish that some other potential prisoners will be able to break out of it into something finer and freer.

The genuine emotion of this sort of middle-aged hope for the hippies was eloquently expressed by Herb Porter, the lawyer on the panel discussion at the "Town Meeting," who defended some of the hippies' unconventional ways to the audience. A young hippie on the panel had tried to describe the rationale of a "love-in" to a hostile questioner, and he said, "It's just letting everybody come and enjoy themselves and enjoy a sunny day, and try to feel like you love everybody, not just your own brother or good friend." There was critical and suspicious questioning about the "loving everybody" business, and fears were expressed about the communal life-styles being experimented with by some of the kids, and it was at this point that Herb Porter said with great sincerity that he would like to respond to some of the questions about this subject.

"I handle a lot of divorce cases," Porter said. "Most of them are middle-class people trying to make it big, trampling on other peoples' feelings and their own. 'Domestic Eight,' where divorces are tried in Los Angeles, is the biggest court of all. We call it 'The War Department.' You have enough hatred exuding into that corridor to move a battleship. I don't care what new approach people are trying—let them try anything. Anything is better than this bitterness which is worse than war itself, and where the children are the battle-ground. Don't belittle anyone who is trying a new approach."

There is this deep sense of the failure of the old social system that makes some of those who have suffered through it and witnessed and experienced its tearings and breakings wish the best for the young hippie experimenters, much in the way that victims of a disease hope that some cure will be discovered that will release those sufferers who follow after them, even if it is too late for their own illness to be healed.

Perhaps that is why so many older people have set up such elaborate machinery to protect the hippies, to try to guarantee them the best possible chance for success in their search, to tend their wounds and supplement their diets. In Haight-Ashbury in San Francisco, there seem to be more agencies to help every possible need of the hippies than to aid any other social minority group on earth, everything from the Hip Medical Clinic and the Hip Job Co-Op to the "Huckleberries" home for—could you guess?—underage runaways.

I spent one evening in Haight-Ashbury at the Hip Switchboard, a coordinating center for receiving all hippie problems and farming them out to the appropriate agency. Mike, a young man in his early thirties already bored and disillusioned with the straight middle-class path set out by the society, but still unable to entirely break with it, was running the operation, helping those who wandered in to the small apartment room as well as those who called. There were other older helpers as well as hippies wandering or plunging in and out, one of the former being Father Grosjean, an Episcopal priest in his thirties who had come to minister to the hippies of Haight-Ashbury.

This was of course the widely advertised "Summer of

Love" in Haight-Ashbury, but the activity at the Hip Switchboard was hardly joyous. A kid called from jail to say he had just been picked up for panhandling, and they found some LSD on him; a young guy came in who said his girl had been picked up for panhandling and he couldn't raise the twenty dollar bill needed to get her out. A call came from a mother who was trying to find her teen-age son who had run away from home after wrecking the car and, over the phone, Mike said "And if we can find him, what's the message?" Then he repeated the message over the phone to the mother, the message being "Please come home—all is forgiven." He promised he would do everything he could to find the boy, and after putting down the phone turned to me and said, "That message—that's what they all say."

Please come home, all is forgiven . . .

A chubby young girl came in, out of breath, and said some Spade had tried to rape her, just a few blocks down the street. Three boys with one guitar and no money came in, looking frightened, and asked if there was any place all of them could crash for the night. A very large, very muscular man with a beard came in with a tall, staring, black-haired girl; they just observed for a while, with wide, wild eyes, and when Mike asked what he could do for them the man said they were just digging, never mind them, and Mike and Father Grosjean continued talking between calls, but everyone was aware of the eyes, and it was not altogether comfortable. Then there was a sudden "bleep-bleep" sound that seemed to come from inside of Father Grosjean, and he smiled and said it was his wife calling him. That did not seem to entirely explain things, and he drew a small black instrument out from the inside of his coat pocket, which he said was a transmitter that he could be signaled on anywhere within a thirty-mile radius. I had only heard of these devices on television spy shows, but Father Grosjean said you could rent them, and it was very valuable in his work, because he could go out on the street and be anywhere without a phone and yet know that he could still be contacted if he was wanted. Father Grosjean said he'd better go see what was up, which left me and Mike with the big guy and his girl with the eyes.

The guy said he lived in the Haight and wanted to help the switchboard if he dug it, and then he started talking very fast, and loud, about how a friend of his had been arrested the week before in a big bust in the neighborhood, there had been a hassle with the fuzz, and this girl he knew went to the police station, she had been beaten he said by the fuzz and her hand was bleeding, and then he started shouting, "And you know how she signed the police register, when they asked her to sign her name? She stamped her bloody palm on it, and left the blood for her signature! The blood, the blood! Her name!"

He smashed his fist into the palm of his hand, over and over, and then started talking of other things and pacing around the room, and said that what the switchboard needed was a real switchboard not just a couple of telephones, and he would get them one, he could get it, never mind, and finally he and the girl left and Mike sighed with some relief and said to me, "He was high on speed. And he was really going fast."

It was the Summer of Love in Haight-Ashbury. It showed, among other things, what ought to have been very obvious even to those who were rooting for the hippies: that painting the word Love on the forehead does not necessarily bring about an interior change in a human being.

It wasn't just the Haight-Ashbury, of course, that made many hippie rooters less hopeful about the joys of dropping

out and turning on. Back in Cambridge, Mass., after returning from California, I talked with a girl in her late twenties
who had moved a little into the hippie fringe and found that
pot was just terrific, but still was, at her late twentyish age,
somewhat shocked by some of the younger seekers. I was
telling this very pretty young girl, you know, that it was
pretty definite that LSD could cause birth defects in the
children of women who had used it a lot. She just shrugged
and said, "So what? The children will be screwed-up anyway."

ii. *Young editors assemble and hear their Che Guevara discuss tactics against the administration; the author suggests
that elders beware the Generation Gap*

Editors of college newspapers from all over the country
came to a conference of the United States Student Press Association at the Minneapolis campus of the University of Minnesota, and held a number of enlightening and entertaining
sessions that dealt with many of their common problems, the
seemingly predominant one being how to avoid all controls
and influences that might be exercised over them by their
administrations and faculties.

Strategies and tactics for dealing with the battle against
the oppressive hand of academic elders and authority figures
were bluntly kicked around at one evening session devoted
to what the editors called the problem of "Co-opting Out."
This is a favorite new term which has replaced the formerly
popular "selling out," the latter term perhaps no longer being
valid because in the current youth ambience, "selling" is
such a distasteful concept, and so repugnant to any respectable person that it is hardly worth discussing. One cannot be

bought, but one still might be in danger of being "co-opted," without even knowing it. The subtleties of the process make it especially important to be on guard.

The leading authority on this issue was Ray Mungo, who might be best described as the Che Guevara of college and now postgraduate journalistic circles. Mungo had just completed a revolutionary year of editorship of the undergraduate paper of Boston University, during which he had seemingly set a record for outraging the authorities, as well as the more conservative or traditional segment of the student body, and had managed to do it without ever being shut down or kicked out of school.

Ray is a very small guy physically, looking to be not much more than one hundred pounds with typewriter included, but he can frighten anyone over thirty. He slouches down in his chair and into his denim suit that he wears most of the time, and looks out from black-rimmed glasses beneath a shock of long brown hair that covers a lot of his forehead, and he puffs on a cigarette and intersperses most of his conversation with words like gas, and groove, and shit, and drag, and it is all very casual and with it.

Mungo was on the stage for this panel discussion talking informally about how you resist co-opting out, based on his own quite impressive record of avoiding such perils during his year of editorship, which included campaigns to abolish the ROTC, impeach Lyndon Johnson, endorse black power, and challenge the Massachusetts birth control law.

When one assumes editorship of the paper, Mungo warned, one is liable to be invited out by the president of the university and subjected to various co-opting techniques, and it is necessary to be on constant guard and not fall into the trap of flattery and false camaraderie.

"The thing to do is hold back and be very cold, be very

detached from the whole bag," Mungo explained. "What happens is, or what happened with me was, that the president invited me out for dinner and fed me all this gin, and called me Ray and everything, and gave me all this advertising-type bullshit, like, 'Well, you just throw out your questions, Ray, and I'll reel them in.' Shit like that. I mean, go ahead and drink his gin, he's paying for it, but don't get sucked in."

Mungo noted that he had got the right start psychologically with the president because the first time he had an appointment to see him, even before the dinner, it was sometime in the morning, and Ray had been up late and he slept through the appointment.

"I just called up his secretary and told her I was sorry I missed the appointment, but I was asleep. That's a good move."

Then the dean of students wanted to see him, and Mungo said he went and nodded through what the dean had to say without really agreeing with anything, and then, "At the end, he pulled this old co-opting trick that they all try to pull. He said, 'Well, Ray, have we learned anything from each other today, and can we trust each other?' I told him no, I had heard all that shit before and I didn't learn anything at all and I didn't trust him. After that he didn't bother me anymore."

There were, however, some university employees that it was well to treat with respect. For instance, when cafeteria workers and janitors had a strike the paper supported it and urged students not to cross the picket lines. This is a sound political move, because, Ray said, "When you get the janitors on your side you can really screw up a university."

Someone in the audience asked Mungo just how far he thought the editor of a college paper should go in challenging the administration, and he answered with a big grin, "I'm in favor of breaking all the laws possible that you can get away with. And do it arrogantly, so they can't accuse you of being sly."

The audience was now breaking up with laughter and applause, for even those editors who thought Mungo far too radical in politics and editorial approach were getting a kick out of the thing. It was like a Negro audience hearing Rap Brown put down the honkies, even though a lot of them might have been "moderates."

It was asked if this concentration on controversy lost advertising, and Mungo told how that worked.

"I had this business manager who was a very capitalistic cat," he said; "I mean he wanted the ads coming in. But when I asked him how the campaigns affected the ads he said, 'Look, you lose some, you gain some.' That's about it. Like in one campaign we had on something controversial we lost an ad from a right-wing deli, but we gained an ad from a union."

Somebody said he got the idea that Mungo wasn't just trying to present the issues but was trying to influence how people felt about them.

"Sure I was trying to convince people," he said, "and I did. At the end of the year the government department took a survey of the freshman class and senior class. They found that only thirty-five percent of the seniors agreed with our editorials but seventy-five percent of the freshmen did. The freshmen's minds were malleable, and this was the first time they'd ever heard the anti-establishment side of things, and we convinced them."

The influence of a student paper on another campus was explained by Tony Gittens, who had served as features editor of the *Hilltop,* student paper of Howard University. Like most Negro institutions of higher learning, Howard had been largely "pacified" as far as protest against the establishment was concerned, but there, as at B.U. and other places, the paper shook things up a bit or at least was an important factor.

"The Howard paper last year created an atmosphere of militancy on the campus," Tony said. "We had editorials against the war in Vietnam, and in support of black power. The administration was surprised by the black-power editorial. In it we said it was time for the students to start acknowledging they are black and stop trying to be bourgeois."

When General Hershey had come to speak on the campus there was a big demonstration of protest against the draft and Tony said that "members of the paper's editorial staff were among the leaders" of the protest. Not only had the paper added militancy but also, Tony said, "We stopped publishing a lot of public relations garbage."

At the end of the year Tony and twenty others were dismissed from the university, and he said that in the next academic year some of them were going to start in Washington their own independent paper off campus which would serve the black community of D.C. as well as the students at Howard. "We decided this was the only way to get around cooptation," he said.

Tony said he thought the administration wanted a fraternity-type person to edit the college paper, which seems now to be the symbol of the establishment's representative on the student body at many colleges. An editor on the panel from the Cornell *Daily Sun* reported that his own administration had similar longings for the good old days when Joe College fraternity boys ran the publications.

"At Cornell," he said, "we alienated every part of the administration, both through our news coverage and our editorials. Well, they couldn't kick us out, so they put out a rival paper, a house organ really, and—*get this*—it was edited and written by the interfraternity council!"

The very notion of fraternity men putting out a newspaper seemed hilarious to most of the audience. Like, how square could you get?

"Naturally," the Cornell *Sun* man assured them, "the thing they put out was so bad it only served to raise our prestige."

In discussion from the floor it was generally agreed by panelists and others that in fighting the administration the faculty was sometimes helpful but couldn't be counted on— "especially the liberals," who will seem to befriend you but will often side with the administration when it comes to a real confrontation.

One editor asked if this wasn't kind of unfair, plotting against the administrations and talking about all these strategies and so on, and there were hoots and boos and quickly Mungo said they did the same thing, and Tony from Howard said: "Listen, I used to be very naïve and believe in the morality of the system. But black people are getting hip to that now. You think the administrators don't get together and plot against students? Only last year a group of black university presidents had a conference at some place in Virginia, and don't you think they discussed this sort of thing?"

"That's right" said Mungo, "I was asked to address a meeting of university administrators last year. Of course they get together—and I didn't get to sit in and listen to what they were saying either. I just had to speak and leave."

It was obvious that most of the editors were in favor of this kind of strategy discussion and pooling of experience and tactics. A young man from Queens College who said he had been put on disciplinary probation because of things he had written in the paper said he thought this sort of thing was extremely valuable and could help college editors all over the country in their effort to stay unfettered and independent. "Here, tonight," he pointed out, "we're getting expertise."

✦   ✦   ✦

Anybody for President
—sign carried at a love-in

✦   ✦   ✦

The college editors were not all hippie, but most seemed very "hip" in the now old sense of the term, meaning knowing what was going on and how to make things happen and how not to be conned, not just by the college administration but by any other figure of authority. Seeing the editors more than seeing the out-and-out hippies made me feel that the Generation Gap was indeed a reality, and that elders like General Lewis Hershey, and Lyndon B. Johnson, and Ronald Reagan, as well as all the college presidents and the college recruiters for corporations (not just Dow Chemical) might as well get used to it.

C. *The tanks and snipers on the tv screen are not in Santo Domingo but in Newark and Detroit; blacks revolt in the street, and the search for "brotherhood" is replaced by the search for "power"; well-meaning white liberal do-gooders (honkies) need not apply*

i. *The Poverty War is even more unpopular than the Vietnam War; I ride with the fuzz; looting lessons on television*

The only declared war being fought by the United States is the War on Poverty. The President declared it in 1964, and it continues to be waged. Unlike the war in Vietnam, the War on Poverty does not cost very much to fight. Even so, it is not a popular war, and in fact is even less popular politically than the war in Vietnam, which must make it *the* most unpopular war in the nation's history. In the Congress that followed the summer of the greatest civil strife in the cities' ghettos, the representatives of the people voted to cut the budget of the War on Poverty, even though its annual cost was set at just a little over $2 billion, which is only about one fifteenth of what it costs to fight the war in Vietnam for a year.

Like the war in Vietnam, the War on Poverty seems to have no end in sight, but in both cases the President keeps predicting victory. Just as he went to see the Vietnam War at firsthand and said once while he stood on a battleship that it surely couldn't last "many more nights" if everyone pulled together, so he also went to see the War on Poverty and assured the men fighting in it that victory would be theirs. A story in the Los Angeles *Times* during the summer of the greatest civil strife told how the President had "toured one of the most successful fronts" in the Poverty War and "predicted victory." At a job-training center in Philadelphia, the President told Poverty warriors, "I think we are going to make it." Just as he found high morale among the troops in the unpopular Vietnam War, he also found dedication and devotion among the troops engaged in the unpopular Poverty War, and he said after touring the "front" in Philadelphia: "I have seen men and women whose self-respect is beginning to burn inside them like a flame—like a furnace that will fire them all their lives."

But those were not the only fires and flames that were set among poor people that summer. The War on Poverty began and was intended to be fought as a cold war in which money, psychology, food, medicine, and education would be the weapons. It was not at all anticipated that a War on Poverty would become a hot war waged with tanks and guns. But that is what happened. The poor people started it, and the government naturally had to respond to aggression in its own streets just as it did in Southeast Asia or the Dominican Republic, and so it sent military troops and armor to quell the insurgency. In the summer that the President saw the flames of self-respect burning inside men and women, there were flames from violent uprisings of poor people in thirty-two different cities across the nation, and nearly one hundred Negroes were killed in the fighting. (Not all the poor are Negroes, but almost all the Negroes are poor.)

This was indeed a War on Poverty, for in the uprisings the poor people burned and looted buildings and stores and took home many nice things that they were too poor to buy. The acquisition of these goods certainly increased the standard of living of some of the people, but this was not what the government meant by a War on Poverty.

The nation was alarmed at this civil strife, and as in every important crisis, the government responded by appointing a commission to study the problem. That is what the government had done two years before after the riots in the Los Angeles ghetto called Watts, and the commission, headed by John A. McCone, said in its report:

"The existing breach, if allowed to persist, could in time split our society irretrievably. So serious and so explosive is the situation that unless it is checked, the August riots [in Watts in 1965] may seem by comparison to be only a curtain-raiser for what could blow up in the future."

The commission's analysis was correct. It was so correct that after the increasing numbers of riots that followed in the ensuing two summers, the government had to appoint another commission.

The new commission, called the President's Advisory Commission on Civil Disorders, was charged with finding the "causes" of the riots. Presumably, it would find much the same things that the McCone Commission had found two years before, and would warn of the future disasters in just as imperative language. However, the new commission used up the $850,000 it had been granted for its work and needed another $2 to $3 million to complete the study before the *next* summer's riots began, requiring still another commission to study the problem with all the fresh material that would doubtless be available at the new summer's end.

To an outsider, unaccustomed to the way things are done

in a supernation, all this might seem odd. Among the many curious aspects of it might be the seemingly large amounts of money required to study the problem. For researchers without access to such funds, I can recommend an experience which gives a real sense of the situation in the large city ghetto where riots have occurred, and might make the whole thing more understandable. Such an experience can be gained by spending an evening riding around with the police in one of the ghetto areas as they go about their ordinary rounds. It costs nothing at all. Sometimes the police stop for coffee, but it is customary in large cities for policemen to be served their coffee "on the house," and this courtesy applies to people who are accompanying them. So all it really costs is the carfare to get to the police station, which is bound to be less than $850,000, even if you pick a police station on the other side of the country.

✦ ✦ ✦

> By every reliable index, America will be living with its new style of normalcy for some time to come. . . . In Los Angeles, for example, the cops are experimenting with a 20-ton armored personnel carrier that can tote twenty fully-equipped men and boasts a .30 caliber machine gun, tear-gas launchers, a smoke screen device, chemical fire extinguishers, hoses and a siren so high-powered that its wail can temporarily stun rioters. "When I look at this thing," says one L.A. police planner, "I think, My God, I hope we never have to use it. But we might as well be prepared."
> —Newsweek, *November 20, 1967*

✦ ✦ ✦

The First Precinct in Detroit covers a downtown area that is largely Negro in population and has one of the highest crime rates in the city. It had not been one of the worst hit areas of the city's insurrection that had left thirty dead, an estimated 1,100 wounded, and some $200 million in damages, but it had a fair share of burning and looting, and if not entire blocks there were individual stores and buildings left in ruin, like the pictures you see of cities that have been subjected to aerial bombardment. As well as the regular police squad cars on duty every night, there is for this as for each of the other precincts in the city one police car called an "elite cruiser" that responds to and looks for any special trouble, and, as one of its crew explained, "handles anything to do with shootings, holdups, guns, mostly crimes of violence." One Friday night in the month after the great rebellion or riot I reported to the First Precinct headquarters in order to spend a routine weekend evening on tour with the men of Cruiser #1.

The precinct station was much the same as those everywhere, the rather dim lobbylike atmosphere and the bulletin boards with pictures of Most Wanted Criminals and the high desklike partition behind which sits the sergeant who books the arrested citizens as they are brought in. Among the other signs and mementos serving as decorations was a plaque on the wall of the main room with a quote from Theodore Roosevelt that said, "Aggressive fighting for the right is the best sport the world affords."

Around 9:15 I met the men of Cruiser #1, whose leader was a soft-spoken, personable man named Bill, who wore a plain brown suit with three ball-point pens clipped to the left breast pocket, a brown tie, and a white shirt with slightly frayed cuffs. The rest of the crew was composed of Stan, a balding veteran of nineteen years on the force, dressed a little more casually than Bill in a plaid sport coat and open-necked yellow sport shirt and black slacks, and Jim, who had on his blue police uniform and looked as if he might have been a linebacker in pro football who had put on a little weight since his playing days. Jim drove the car and Stan rode with him in front while Bill and I sat in back. Bill explained that these cruisers used to have four-man crews but owing to the manpower shortage were reduced to three. As another "plainclothesman," I felt like, and was taken to be by the citizens whom we encountered, the fourth man of the crew.

There was no immediate crisis as we started out, and so Bill suggested that we look around for a Negro woman named May who had reportedly stabbed her latest boyfriend to death and was believed to be in hiding in the area. Bill showed me the mug shot of "May," who had short fuzzy hair and a blank expression, which evidently hid certain violent tendencies, for Jim said, "This is the second guy she's knocked off." We pulled up on a dark, quiet street of two- and three-story houses where some people were sitting out on a porch, and Bill picked up the big silver flashlight that each of the men carried and beamed it around the faces. The beam stopped on one ragged-looking young woman, and Bill said, "Hey, you, c'mere."

She came to the car, and Bill held the beam on her face and then on the mug shot and showed it to her and asked if she knew this May, or where she was. First the girl peered in the car and said, "Y'all's new ones, ain't ya?" and they said no, and she said, "Oh, thas right, you're the ones gimme a break."

Stan asked if she was hustling anymore, and she said, oh, no, she had given that up for good, and Stan asked, well how was she living then, and she said she had friends, and Stan laughed and said they must be *good* friends. Questioned some more, she first said she didn't know of this May, and then pressed further said, yes, maybe she did, maybe she was the May who'd been hanging around the corn-likker place. The car cruised off then, and the men chuckled about this girl they had just questioned, and Jim explained, "She's a guy."

The "corn-likker place" was suspected of being a "Blind Pig," an unlicensed place to buy drinks (the ghetto night-club) in a private apartment. This one (we entered two others during the evening) was a single dim room with an Americana jukebox and a couch and some chairs and about a dozen guys sitting around who of course fell silent when we came in. Of course there were no drinks in sight and no evidence that such purchases were being made. Jim flashed his light on each face, asked a few for ID's, and read the name of one as "Joe Springer." Jim turned to Bill, and said, "Do we want a Joe Springer?" and Bill said he didn't think so, and no one knew anything about May and we left.

Perhaps naïvely, it seemed to me unlikely that the black citizens were going to give these white cops any hot information leading to the arrest of May, but they seemed undismayed, even though Bill admitted that their best informers in the neighborhood, the reliable ones, were in jail because of the riot. Some woman on a street corner where we stopped said May was hiding out with Big Joe, and that he had a room at Mary's place, and so we went there. It was a three-story rooming house, and some of the residents were in a darkened living room watching television. Mary got up, and after a great deal of looking at her rent records and wondering what it was all about said, oh, yes, Big Joe was in Room 17 on the third floor.

Jim had to stay in the car in case any emergency calls came over the radio, so Bill and Stan and I charged up the flights of stairs. Stan drew a pistol, and as we were chugging up, looked back over his shoulder and reminded me I was not to take part if there was any action. I said I understood, and I privately hoped that if we found Big Joe he would understand too. Bill knocked on the door, and a female voice asked who it was, and Bill affected a Negro drawl and said, "It's me, honey, Joe." There was a lot of sounds of shuffling and the woman inside was mumbling things and then Bill said in the same accent, "It's *Po*-leece, open up," and still there was more activity inside and Stan ran downstairs to position himself outside the window in case she tried to get rid of some heroin or other illegal drug, and finally she opened the door.

There was this tiny Negro woman, around eighty pounds, wearing just a pajama top and a black bra and white panties and frayed gold house slippers, and she started at once denying everything, whatever it might be. The room was papered in a sickly green, with gaping patches of white plaster over it, and there was a large iron bed and an old TV set that was playing and a broken-down dresser with a vast array of partly used cosmetics and potato chips on it. Bill picked up a rumpled pink blanket from the bed, and a dozen or so hypodermic needles fell out. The woman said she didn't have any idea how those got there, she was just visiting there for the night. Bill rolled up the sleeves of her pajamas to see if there were any needle marks, but there were only some old ones which the woman said she got back in high school.

Bill started searching the room, and the woman said to me, " 'Scuse me for being dressed like this, I was just havin' a beer and watchin' TV." Bill pulled something out of the overflowing wastebasket and said, "Are you by any chance having your period?" She said she was. Bill asked if her name was May, and she said no, her name was Mary. Bill showed her the mug shot of May, and said it looked a lot like her, and she said no, it didn't, and there was a big wrangle about identification which finally was settled by the evidence that May had a front tooth missing and this woman opened her mouth and Bill examined her teeth. None of them were missing or false, and so Bill accepted the fact that she was not May. She said no, she wasn't, her name was Janet. Bill said he thought it was Mary, and she said no it was Janet Mc-Mary. Bill went to the closet and pulled out a shotgun, and the woman said she certainly didn't know anything about *that*. Underneath the bed he found a syringe and some more needles and some razor blades, which he explained to me were for dividing portions of heroin, and this was definitely a "shooting pad" for making connections.

"Those razors," the woman said, "are just for cutting off my corns."

Stan yelled something from downstairs outside, and Bill told the woman to get dressed. She said that there wasn't nothing *on* her, she was just bein' arrested for *visitin'*, that's no crime, and could she take her beer with her? Bill said she better hurry up, and added in a very restrained, quiet voice, "Don't get me mad—I don't like to get mad. I get mad at myself when I get mad."

The woman hurried up, and Bill continued poking around the room and pulled some .38 caliber bullets out of a drawer which he showed me, and the woman said, "I can't help no bullets. I'm just visitin'."

We walked downstairs with her, and the people who had been watching TV were now gathered around looking at us, and the woman said to the landlady, "Tell him you know me, tell him I'm Julia Carter and you know me and I'm just visitin'." The landlady didn't say a word and just looked at her with huge sorrowful eyes and then closed them. Outside in the car it turned out that Bill had thought Stan had found some stuff the gal had thrown out the window, but he hadn't found anything and so there was no ground for holding her, and Bill told her to go on back, and she said, "How come you're not takin' me in?" and Bill said is that what she wanted, and she said no, and so she got out and went back to the porch, where all those eyes were fixed on us, silent, no one saying a word.

We cruised around some more and passed a boarded-up restaurant that Jim said was burned to the ground inside during the riots. The place was the Checker Barbecue, and Jim said, "It had all colored employees, too, and still they burned it. White fella owned it. Jewish fella." Bill shook his head and said, "They served the best ribs in town."

A call came over the radio saying that a motorcycle gang was heading for Plum Street, the hippie center, and a big crowd was already in the streets there. A big dance was going on at the Emporium on Plum Street, and the motorcycle guys as well as the hippies were there, but no one was breaking any laws and so we cruised on after taking in the street scene of longhairs and leather-jacket guys.

"I tell ya," Stan said, "they ought to send a lot of those bastards to Vietnam. Let 'em get a little taste of it."

We stopped at street corners, asking about May again, and the men inquired about other people in the neighborhood. At one corner it was learned that a local called Prince was in the bughouse, and an hour or so later we happened on a group of young Negroes who were being searched by two police from a regular squad car who were checking out a report of somebody having been rolled, and Bill said, "Hey, that's Prince's brother." Jim pulled the car up, and Bill rolled down the window and said, "Hey, where's Prince?" The guy who was his brother said, "He's sick." Bill laughed, and said, "Not too good in the head, huh?" Prince's brother didn't answer, and Bill said, "He's in the nuthouse, huh?" There was silence, and then Prince's brother said very slowly, very deeply, the separate words sounding as if they might break or explode:

"He has never been so happy in his life."

Bill chuckled and rolled the window back up and we cruised off, down the dark, tree-lined streets of quiet houses.

We came across two young white boys on a deserted street who had just been victimized by the Murphy game. That is where someone tells them that he can take them to this great whorehouse, and they can have any woman they want, but first he has to have their money, and he writes down what kind of woman (white, black, Chinese, and so on) they want on a slip of paper and goes to "make the arrangements" and never comes back. The two nice-looking young white boys said that between them they had given the guy $115. They didn't want to report it though because it would be on their records and they were applying for college the next year, and, as one of them put it, "We don't want it on our record that we were trying to get laid."

We drove past a movie house with a marquee that proclaimed "Weird World of LSD" and "Faster Pussycat Kill Kill" and a bar that said "Female Impersonators—America's Finest," and the Detroit City Rescue Mission with a marquee that said "Christ Died for Our Sins" and The Fine Arts Theatre advertising "Infidelity American Style Plus Run Swinger Run & Hot Rocks." We passed a dilapidated building with a weather-beaten poster on it that said, "UAW Seeks Justice and Equality," and another that said, "Judge Crockett—Outstanding." We stopped a young Negro guy whom Jim recognized, and he called him over to the car and said, "You know what'll happen to you if we catch you rollin' somebody again?" The guy said, "I'll go to jail," but that was not the right answer. Jim munched on the big cigar he was constantly smoking or chewing on, and he said, "What'll happen is, I'll kick your head right off your shoulders." We stopped at a restaurant for coffee, and then at a drugstore so Bill could get some empty cigar boxes for his son to make into a fishing tackle box; he had promised to take his son fishing, but then the riots came and all vacations were canceled, but maybe soon there'd be a chance. We chased some kids believed to be smoking pot out of the playground by Brewster Center, where Joe Louis used to train, and we stopped two young men on suspicion of a robbery that came over the radio, and one of the young men said he had just got back from Vietnam and was thinking of signing up again. Bill said, "You crazy or something?" and the guy smiled and said, "I like the life," seemingly better than the one on this particular corner. We went into another Blind Pig and no one knew the whereabouts of May or Big Joe there either and we pulled up at a luncheonette where Jim said, "I'm gonna chase me some kids," and he caught a couple of kids about ten years old and found a pack of Kools on one of them and took out the cigarettes and ripped them apart and threw them in the gutter and told the kids to get on home. Bill remarked that it had been a very quiet Friday night, and Jim said, "Maybe it's this cool weather has something to do with it. They don't like to get too chilly."

✦ ✦ ✦

A SOFT SUMMER NIGHT

The proposition was offered that the United States of America had gone crazy; there were natural patriotic objections; and then a man finally said: "If this country hasn't gone crazy, then just why in the hell are we sitting in the South Bronx right across from

a truck the police have rented just in
case they might have to answer a distress call and might get shot before
they get there if they were recognized
by a fellow citizen?"

—*Murray Kempton, the New York*
Post

❖ ❖ ❖

Most of the police in the large city ghettos are white, and
they are mostly regarded as occupying troops by the black
residents, and in turn their attitudes are those of colonial
legionnaires overseeing the natives. This racial aspect of the
urban wars is certainly significant, and yet there is also a
strong purely "poverty" strain in it all that lures the poor
whites in these areas to join their black neighbors in what is
really "integrated looting." A Negro woman in Detroit who
lived two doors from a warehouse that was looted and
burned told a reporter there were whites as well as blacks in
on the action, and so it was really not a "race riot." "It's an
all of 'em riot," she explained.

A white woman who lived across the street and watched
the pillage of the warehouse confirmed that view to the press,
and added that the integrated rioters got along just fine:
"They were laughing, talking, having a good time. It seemed
like everyone was enjoying themselves." So the riots, in Detroit at least, did what all the radical organizations had failed
to do—brought the poor of both races together in a common
cause, made them see that the enemy was not race but class
and they should be battling together for what they needed,
instead of against each other.

These people *do* share a deep bond beyond difference of
color, for they are common victims of what must be one of
the most frustrating positions in history; being have-nots in
a society that seems to have everything and unlike former

lord-and-serf societies in which the order was taken to be in the nature of things, in this society they are taunted by not having all the best, the latest sleek car and fine mink lounging pajamas and color TV's and washing machines and all of the incredible effluvia of the cornucopia filled by the richest country in the history of the world. You see how "the other half lives"; in fact, you are taken into the very living rooms of the rich and powerful by the magic of television, and the ads you see say that the wonderful products offered, the luxury vacations in Caribbean islands, the mighty new automobiles, the sleek, jeweled women are for *you*, Mr. Viewer, not just the lords, but all of you out there in videoland.

Consider how it must feel not to have any of it; to see it and hear about it every day and not be able to touch it, and how fine an emotional thing it must be to smash the glass that separates it from your rightful possession as a citizen of this most affluent land, and to push and drag, as the poor of both races did in Detroit, the gleaming appliances up over curbs and through peoples' yards and into your own home where it surely belongs. In discussing the passion of these things with the Vice President of the United States, I asked if he didn't think this teasing sort of lure on television added to some of the force behind the lootings, and he said, "Oh, my yes, why, did you know that they found that the things the people took from the stores were the ones that were most advertised? They took the TV's or the stoves or whatever that had been best promoted in TV and papers and magazine ads. Why, the way the people selected those things they looted was the greatest triumph of advertising the world has ever seen!"

As the bounty groans and gleams all around, it is only natural that people want to take it, and in fact that natural instinct is shown every weekday on television. There is a program called Supermarket Sweep, in which three teams, each composed of a nice young husband and wife, are given a grocery cart and set loose for a certain limited time in a supermarket, and the team that stuffs the greatest amount of goodies, worth the most money, and returns first to the checkout counter is the winner. The studio audience squeals and cheers as the great steaks and roasts and frozen delicacies and gourmet foods are stuffed into the carts as they madly career through the aisles in a frenzy of acquisition. It is a fantasy acted out, a form of legalized looting as entertainment. Who has not entered a great supermarket and not imagined doing just that, being alone with all the carts and wheeling out everything you wanted? No wonder the program has great appeal.

There is of course one flaw for identification purposes of the whole viewing audience. In the dozen or so times I watched the show (always with fascination), there were never any Negro couples. In the subconscious of the general white public, it might seem too much like real looting if the goods were grabbed by the blacks. The NAACP might even object to having Negroes participate in such a televised pillage on the grounds that it might be bad for their image.

And think how it would look if a Negro couple won.

---

ii. *Colored turns to black, including the decline of the Knee-grow; power and violence prove popular, but civil disobedience is hard to sell*

Until the development of the civil rights movement beginning in the late 1950's, most white people used the word "colored" to refer in a polite and respectful way to the darker people whom they referred to in jokes or other non-respectful conversation as "niggers." They also sometimes used the nonrespectful term "black," as in "I was walkin'

down Main Street and this big black buck came strollin'
along just as sassy as you please . . ." The word "colored" was
really a kind of avoidance, "polite" because it didn't come
out and say more specifically what was being referred to,
which was not nice. But with civil rights, the more advanced
of the "colored" wished to be more specifically identified as
"Negro"; that was, after all, the official name given to their
race, and they felt they should not be ashamed of it. This was
a little hard for well-meaning whites to adjust to, for the
word was so much like the bad word "nigger" that one had
to be very careful pronouncing it and many had to stop and
concentrate to be sure it came out "Knee-grow," so that it
couldn't possibly be thought to have sounded like "nigger."

The Southern accent had particular difficulty pronouncing
the word "Knee-grow," and there developed a genteel Southern white version of the word, which was "nigra," a hybrid
pronunciation that contained an element of the old familiar
"nigger" and yet made a definite concession to the new, more
respect-demanding "Knee-grow." Like many Southern customs, the pronunciation was a dramatic one, leaving the listener still in a state of suspense halfway through the word
since the first syllable of both "nigger" and "nigra" were the
same and not till the final sound came out could the listener
know by the "ger" or the "gra" how the speaker felt about
these matters.

And then like many ironic tricks played on the white well-
meaning liberal, just about the time he had mastered a
fluency in pronouncing the word "Knee-grow," when he had
become so practiced that it almost flowed right along in the
conversation instead of sticking out like an awkward bump
in an otherwise smooth sentence, just about the time this
thing was mastered it became obsolete. Foiled again. When
the latest racial revolutionaries linked the word "black" with
the word "power" the word "black" suddenly became not

only acceptable but desirable as a term of identity of which the bearer should be proud. Historians of the movement pointed out that "Knee-grow" was only a word invented by the white man and so never had any validity anyway, and also there was a nice kind of mockery and turn of the tables in adopting as a term of pride the word that in most of its citations in dictionaries (which were written by whites) stood for all sorts of evil things just the opposite of the word "white." *"We are making the whole idea of the word different just like the whole idea of ourselves, and the meaning you gave to both is no longer true, you had it wrong all along, you stupid pale-faced bigots"*—so could the new black man say by simply insisting on proudly calling himself and his brothers black.

It caught on very quickly, the honky whites got the word, not only in political circles but in sports and popular magazines. An article about pro football in *Look* magazine in the fall of 1967 referred offhandedly to "the black players" on a certain team. Two years before, the same term in the same article would have sounded shockingly like racism. Now it was respect.

❖   ❖   ❖

SEGREGATION BEGAN AT BABEL
by David Otis Fuller, Pastor, Wealthy Street Baptist Church, Grand Rapids, Michigan
. . . . When I was in the Navy as chaplain in World War II stationed at Long Beach, N. Y., there were two barracks of colored sailors. . . . How those colored fellows did sing and enjoy themselves! One of them I led to Christ there on the base. I'll never forget him—a great big colored fellow named Emerson Ragsdale. He had been before captain's mast countless times. He defied the captain, standing there with a sneer on his face. I called him in one day, dealt with him, got him down on his knees and that 200-pound colored fellow accepted

Christ. Several weeks later I met him on the parade ground.
My jaw almost dropped, he seemed so changed. I said "Ragsdale, what happened?" "Ah guess Ah got saved, Chaplain."
  —*from a pamphlet distributed in Grand Rapids during the
riot in the Negro section in the summer of 1967*

✦ ✦ ✦

Most police, and in fact most white people, refer to the
ghetto violence as "riots," although there are some modifica-
tions. Grand Rapids, Michigan, had a small or "mini-riot,"
which one police officer there in attempting to minimize its
impact, delicately referred to as "the days of the trouble"
and then smiled and said, "Oh, hell, that sounds like the
Irish Rebellion." But to many of the blacks of the ghettos,
the "troubles" or "disturbances" to the society at large were
a source of pride and are described as "revolts."

That is the attitude in Watts, the southeast Los Angeles
ghetto area which erupted in 1965 with a revolt that cost
thirty-four lives, 1,000 buildings burned, and some $20 mil-
lion in property damage. Those who "revolted" were proud
of the fact that they had defeated their worst enemy, the L.A.
Police Department, which had to call for help from the National Guard. Those who took part are veterans and local
heroes; young men of the neighborhood still proudly flash
the three-finger sign that means "Burn." Out of the rubble
came a new sense of identity and pride and new organizations and leaders, among whom the most militant and articulate is a twenty-six-year-old man named Ron Karenga, who is
the founder and leader of a movement called US, which does
not stand for "United States" but simply means "Us," as opposed to "Them." Again this is a nicely ironic turn on the
white man who always thought of the blacks as "Them," and
asked "What do *they* want?" but Karenga turns the tables

and makes himself and his people "US," leaving "Them" to be the whites. Karenga doesn't even give *them* the distinction of being anything as positive as "white." He refers to *them* as "the colorless people."

The US Cultural Center in Watts is on a wide thoroughfare of low, flat-roofed buildings that are occupied by luncheonettes, beauty shops, churches, and furniture stores; the Center itself is in a one-story stucco building that adjoins a dry cleaner's. There is no sign or symbol outside, but once a visitor enters he is struck at once and from many sides by the militant "Afro" ambience. On the face of a large clock on the wall are painted the words "African Time," although it coincided precisely with the "white" time shown on my wristwatch. Two women sat behind desks, typing, one of them wearing a long African-style robe. On the wall were red and black "Malcolm X" sweat shirts, which are very popular among the youth, and also "Ron Karenga" sweat shirts, with the face and name of that new leader, and some of the stickers of the organization were displayed, like ones with the slogans "If You're Not With US, You're in Trouble," and "Just Trying to Be Black." There were signs saying "Black Power" and a poster that showed Uncle Sam holding up a little black boy by the seat of his pants, about to drop him in a red, white, and blue mailbox that was labeled "Vietnam." A man wearing a red tunic, shades, black slacks, and sandals came up and stood in front of me before I could go any further into the room and asked what I wanted. I explained why I was there, and from the back of the room came a short, stocky man dressed like the first man but further distinguished by a shaven head and a mustache that curled down to his chin in the manner of Fu Manchu. He asked me to follow him, and we went into an adjoining room with rows of black seats like church pews and an African mask on the wall at the front. The man opened up two folding chairs for us to sit on and said he was Ron Karenga.

I asked him how his movement differed from other black militant groups, such as, for instance, SNCC, and he explained, "SNCC is all right, but it is *only* political. That's not enough. Our program takes in the areas of culture, history, politics, economics, social organization, and the arts. Many of these things are related. For instance, we are developing our own 'mythology'—what some people would call religion. We are trying to relate it to history, just as the Jewish people have, and we have graduate students working on this. This ties in with the 'religion,' which is very important. We don't believe in the 'spookiness' sort of religious thing, but we have to deal with the emotional needs of our people. We marry our own people, and we are developing our own holidays. 'Uhuru' is the anniversary of the revolt (the one in Watts), and on May nineteenth we celebrate Kuzaliwa, which is the birthday of Malcolm X. We had the children stay away from school this year on Kuzaliwa, and in one school here almost one hundred percent of the children didn't go that day, and the principal had to dismiss classes. Here at the Center we have classes in Swahili, and in Afro-American culture, trying to give the black people a powerful self-image. Of course, we are free from the self-deprecating concept that results from having to worship a white God."

Karenga said that the US economic plans were based on cooperative principles, trying to provide goods and services by and for blacks in a cooperative setup. Yet he felt that economics alone, like politics alone, was meaningless without a whole "value system."

"There are black millionaires, but what good is that without a value system? We have had too much elitism, a philosophy that says once you make it you can forget about your own people. We want to stop this. We have come to kill the individual, and create a collective effort. The white society *identifies* us collectively, so we should *act* collectively. Like the Jews. When Israel went to war with the Arabs, you didn't have Jews there going off into their own individual bag. They were attacked collectively and they *moved* collectively against the enemy. That's what we must do."

I asked if US was a nationwide movement, and how many members it had.

"We will eventually be national in scope. We have contacts and discussion groups in New York, Ohio, Chicago, and Detroit. But first we want to influence things right here in Los Angeles, and in California. We don't keep numbers of membership, and we are stronger than it might seem because we have people in all the significant organizations. In the words of our slogan, "Wherever we are, US is.""

I mentioned the poster in the office about Vietnam, and said I assumed that Karenga did not agree with some Negro (rather than black) leaders like Whitney Young of the Urban League who felt that the war was helpful to the many Negroes who went into the service and received good pay and training in special skills.

Karenga said he thought that the *military* training could be beneficial to blacks—that is, for use in fighting police and national guard in future revolts in the United States, like the one in Watts—but he added that "even if you learn those military skills they're not very beneficial if you get killed in Vietnam, and a lot get killed."

But beyond that consideration he said, "We're against black people fighting in the war. We believe in self-determination, and the United States is not recognizing or allowing the self-determination of the Vietnamese people. Also, we don't believe that we should kill yellow people who are fighting against the white, or what we call 'colorless' people. We want to identify with the 'Third World' of yellow and black people, and we won't be used to help destroy their world."

Though members of US were encouraged not to fight in the war, they were not asked to demonstrate against it or participate in antiwar activities.

"White people should do that work," Karenga said. "That's what liberal whites could go into. Like the demonstration in L.A. against the President where a lot of them got beat up. That was good for them. Now they don't have to ask *us* about police brutality anymore. They should do more of that and they'll have a better idea of the things we encounter every day, and not just on special occasions."

We talked for about forty-five minutes when one of the ladies in the office knocked at the door and reminded Karenga he had to catch a plane. He and a few of his men were going to San Francisco to attend a meeting of CORE, a former civil rights group that had, Karenga assured me, "gone black power."

I followed Karenga into the office, where luggage was being assembled for the trip. I noticed two men in the red tunics of US who were lifting a heavy canvas bag, from which protruded the barrels of a number of rifles. Karenga ordered them to set it down and said he didn't think they should take the sack of rifles on the plane because it might "draw attention." The men reluctantly set the rifles down, obviously disappointed. Karenga rubbed his chin a moment and then solved the dilemma. "Send those Air Freight," he said.

✦ ✦ ✦

The Mafia discriminates against Negroes.
—*a story in the* Wall Street Journal

✦ ✦ ✦

There of course is more to Watts than just "US," and even if Karenga is a hero to many of the residents there, not all of them agree with all his policies. I learned firsthand that some very articulate and talented people in Watts did not, for instance, go along with all of Karenga's ideas about literature. In my talk with him, Karenga had said LeRoi Jones was the first and as yet only truly black writer in America and that James Baldwin was passé because Baldwin's writings "always gave the white man an 'out,' " a sign of weakness that no longer could be tolerated. Suspecting I knew what the answer would be, I nevertheless asked Karenga what he thought of the Watts Writers Workshop taught by Budd Schulberg. Karenga dismissed it with scorn, saying "There's nothing that black people can learn about writing from a white man."

A number of the black residents of Watts evidently didn't agree with that, for when I visited one of the weekly sessions of the Workshop as Mr. Schulberg's guest, the place was packed. Of course, this was after several years of slow and steadily building interest. Schulberg lives in another of the many ghettos of the great city of Los Angeles, the one called Hollywood, and after the riots he went to Watts to offer his own principal talent and the teaching of it to anyone who was interested. The offer would have besieged him with eager acolytes on any college campus with a liberal arts program, but in Watts he had to wait, urge, and coax, for as a stranger from a different ghetto he was held in as much suspicion as if he were an Eskimo attempting to set up a course in igloo architecture, and there seemed about as much demand for instruction in his craft. All this as well as the eventual popularity and productivity of the Writers Workshop has been recounted by Schulberg in the introduction to an anthology of the group's writings called *From the Ashes*.

The Workshop had also produced a nationally televised screenplay of unusual honesty and insight, written by one of the group's members and performed with a cast made up of people from the Workshop.

With contributions from other writers, the Workshop had purchased its own headquarters, a small one-story house in Watts which was christened the Frederick Douglass House, and it was there that I went with Mr. Schulberg to one of the meetings. It happened to be the night when the monthly directors' meeting was held before the general session, and so while Schulberg attended that function I went out to a small house in the backyard where some of the members were reading and discussing their work informally. It was like most other such sessions of aspiring writers, complete with the inevitable practical-minded young man who criticized each work read on the basis of its potential for "the market" of publication. After one slight but rather charming piece was read, the practical young man explained to the author that what she had just read was "what in the market is called 'the vignette,' and there is nothing more difficult to sell in today's market than 'the vignette.' "

Mrs. Ellen Brown, a small, spirited lady who was writing a book, said she would like to read one of the latest chapters. Mrs. Brown explained for those who had not heard previous installments that her book was about a "nice" Negro family; she felt too much was being written about the slums and the problems and hardly anything at all about the nice middle-class families. The part she read concerned the daughter of the "nice" family, a pretty young schoolteacher who kept up with all the latest styles in fashion and politics, as indicated by her wearing white boots and deciding to go to Washington to a civil rights demonstration, all of which led the family to chide her and worry about her, though not in a terribly serious way. The part I heard seemed light and humorous, and pleasantly entertaining. Mrs. Brown's fellow Workshop members were more harsh in their criticism, not about the idea of the story but the execution of the plot, the marketing problems, and other such technical matters of professional concern.

A lady sitting next to me said to the six or eight people assembled that she had a story she would like to read but had left it at home, and she wondered if she might drive over and get it, as she only lived a few blocks away. The group agreed, and I asked the lady if she might let me ride along and get some cigarettes, which I had just run out of. She said that would be fine, and we drove a few blocks to a pleasant, pastel street of houses, one of the many blocks that make the famous "ghetto" areas of the western states seem so much more decent and livable than the tenements of the great eastern cities. The lady told me she had a daughter in college, and that she herself was back in college getting a degree in social work.

"You know, when you say you're from Watts," she explained, "people say, 'Oh my, what's it like living there,' as if you must be having a terrible time just because you live in Watts. People don't know about all the well-off people here, but I guess we shouldn't write about it—at least not yet. I suppose if we did it would hurt the chances of things getting better for those who are less well-off. I mean, it would be bad publicity, I guess."

All American neighborhoods have their own "image" to maintain.

At the main meeting in the living room of Douglass House Mr. Schulberg introduced a special guest speaker who was one of the sponsors of Douglass House, the historical novelist Irving Stone. Mr. Stone talked about his own experiences writing historical novels, and the excitement of working in that particular form, conveying his enthusiasm with such force that I would not have been surprised if everyone present had laid aside his own work and started writing a historical novel. After a question period there was a break for coffee, and I saw Mrs. Brown at the coffee machine and told her I had enjoyed what she'd read from her book at the earlier session.

She thanked me, and asked what I was writing. I said I was traveling around the country and one of my interests was the reaction to the war in Vietnam, which turned out to be a subject on which Mrs. Brown had very strong opinions. She said she had been keeping a scrapbook about the war, and she was plainly angry about the U.S. involvement in it.

"Don't tell me this is a Christian country, fighting that war," she said. "This never *was* a Christian country. Not in action, anyway, just in talk. Do you know what the Pilgrims did when they got here?"

Mrs. Brown paused, and then exclaimed: "First they fell on their knees—then they fell on the Indians!"

Despite this hypocritical aspect of the nation's history, Mrs. Brown said she wasn't necessarily against its wars, and that she did her part when she felt the cause was just.

"You know what I did right after Pearl Harbor? I got a job in a shipyard. I wanted to do my part. But this war now is different, this is not a just cause in Vietnam. We are killing people where it is none of our business."

The meeting was about to resume, and I thanked Mrs. Brown for giving me her opinion, and as we started to walk into the living room she tapped me on the arm and said, "I believe everything I told you, and I don't care if you're from the FBI, you can tell 'em what I said cause that's how I feel!"

I heard how some other members of the Workshop felt about the subject when just before the end of the evening's session Mr. Schulberg introduced me to the whole assembled group—there were now more than twenty people crowded into the living room—and said one of the things I was interested in was the feeling about the war. The first person to speak was the lady I had driven with to pick up her short story.

"I feel we have to support our country," she said. "I feel about it just the way I would if my daughter was pregnant and wasn't married—that it's a bad situation but I'd have to stick by her. When I get my social work degree I intend to go over there and help, because it's my duty. I have a son, and I told him 'you have to go do your duty.' We may have things hard here sometimes but we wouldn't have it better anyplace else in the world, and so we just have to help get this thing over with."

Another middle-aged woman had said earlier that she didn't think Workshop members should take part in the "Angry Artists" demonstrations against the war which were being held in Los Angeles, and she explained that "I don't see anybody demonstrating in Russia, do you? We have more freedom here than we'd have anyplace else and I'm not going to be against our government." This woman's main complaint was: "If so many Negro boys are dying over there, how come they don't show them on TV? Every time I see news about the war, you don't see any Negro boys."

A number of people agreed with this complaint, and then some of the younger men complained about the war itself, most all on variations of the terms put by one who said, "Why should we fight over there when we haven't got our freedom here?"

It seemed in general that the supporters of the war in the

room were the middle-aged people, most of them women (with the exception of Mrs. Brown) while the opponents were the younger men. Driving back after the meeting Schulberg said that breakdown of sentiment was pretty much the way he had seen it among the Workshop members, but he felt some of the younger men were more vehement than they had expressed themselves tonight.

Discussing the militance of many of the young men, Schulberg said that Senator Robert Kennedy had visited Watts some months before, and had asked to meet privately with some of the young people from the Workshop. He wanted a "representative" group, Schulberg said, and "I tried to pick about a half dozen guys who did seem to represent different views, who weren't all completely black power advocates, but who had different ideas and approaches to things. But when I showed up with Kennedy all the young men I'd asked to come were wearing "Malcolm X" sweat shirts. It looked like a football team."

✦ ✦ ✦

"Hey, sock it to me, Black Power, ooh, ah!"
—*a favorite "yell" of the Milwaukee NAACP Youth Council in its marches for open housing in Milwaukee, led by Father James Groppi, a white Roman Catholic Priest*

✦ ✦ ✦

There is a popular saying to the effect that there is nothing so powerful as an idea whose time has come. It would seem just as true, if less noted, that there is nothing so weak and frustrated as an idea whose time has come and gone. By the summer of my travels the "civil rights idea" had come and gone as a means of stirring popular support and action, and the Reverend Martin Luther King, Jr., the principal spokesman and symbol of that idea in America, occupied a very unpopular and lonely position. From one side he was scorned by the militants of the popular new black power idea, and from another side he was attácked by the "moderate" Negro leaders like Roy Wilkins of the NAACP and Whitney Young of the Urban League who criticized King's opposition to the war in Vietnam on the grounds that such criticism hurt the progress of the Negro at home. But King held to his diminishing ground, attempting to find a way of maintaining his relevance as a leader without (and this was the trick, the tightrope requirement) forsaking the very principles on which he had risen to that leadership.

The old civil rights tactics of nonviolent demonstrations and marches that King had led so successfully in the South simply broke down and fizzled out in the streets of Chicago, and King had to confess that "we have not devised the tactics for urban slum reform. We spent ten years in the South using new tactics of nonviolence that were successful. But in the northern cities, with time running out, we failed to achieve creative methods of work. As a result, desperate, essentially leaderless masses of people acted with violence and without a program."

Hemmed in by militant black power and middle-class Negro moderation, King at the end of the "longest, hottest summer" of civil strife convened his Southern Christian Leadership Conference in Atlanta to try to come up with a new and workable answer to the growing revolt of the black masses. The convention was in many ways a sad occasion, and seemed a long way from the triumphal civil rights march on Washington in 1963 when King had a "Dream for America." No talk of dreams was possible now, nor was there the old revival-like spirit of fellowship that marked the meetings in Montgomery and Selma and the civil rights battles of the

South, when it seemed for King's followers that, in the words of the movement's anthem, "Black and white together, we shall overcome."

When the "black power" cry first was raised, King had come out for "human power," which was no longer very appealing in the new mood of racial militance. His own organization, the SCLC, had not cast out the white man, and there were a few, though not many, present at the conference, but they seemed outsiders in a way they never had before in King's campaigns. Though careful not to endorse "black power"—which some observers felt meant the end of King's effectiveness among the masses—King did not make an appeal for working with whites on the old grounds of brotherhood and love and human fellowship, but only on grounds of utility and practical politics. He proposed a plan of civil disobedience that would shut down the essential functions of northern cities, a plan which he hoped would serve as an alternate, nondestructive form of protest to rioting and yet would supply "the social adrenalin of quick change that would be provided by civil disobedience." He argued that "mass civil disobedience can use rage as a constructive and creative force."

In such a program it would be useful to enlist the aid of whites, King said, and he assured the audience that whites would respond, purely as a practical necessity. "Many white decision-makers may care little about saving Negroes, but they must care about saving their cities. The vast majority of production is created in the cities; most white Americans live in them; the suburbs, to which they flee, cannot exist detached from the central cities. Hence powerful white elements objectively have goals that merge with ours."

There was no mention of moral or ethical reasons for whites taking part in such action, only the "objective" factor of mutual benefit from working for practical goals that happened to merge. The "Dream for America" was now a technical battle plan, based not on brotherhood but self-interest. There was no reason to believe that the Reverend King had himself forsaken any of those former ideals that fired the civil rights movement of old, but there was every reason to believe that in the new racial atmosphere he could no longer invoke such concepts or suggest any grounds other than utilitarian for cooperating with whites if he wanted to keep any hope of being heard by the black masses.

It was dangerous enough for King to stop short of endorsing the new black version of segregation, and also to face the fire from the moderate side by refusing, as he put it, to "segregate my moral conscience" on the issue of Vietnam. He cited the war as one of the causes of the urban rioting, saying that "Negroes are not only conscripted in double measure for combat, but they are told the billions needed for remaking their lives are necessary for foreign intervention. . . . The immoral, insane pursuit of conquest against the will of the people has to diminish respect for government."

King defended his outspoken criticism of Vietnam by claiming, "I am not a consensus leader. . . . I don't determine what is right and wrong by looking at the budget or taking a poll. A genuine leader is not a searcher for consensus, but a molder of consensus."

It remained to be seen how much King could mold the masses with his new plan of civil disobedience that stopped short of revolt and stopped short of black power rhetoric. One side of the dilemma was forcefully and frankly stated in a talk by a brilliant young Negro woman named Barbara Jordan, who is a member of the Texas State Legislature and speaks with the grace and style and even a bit of the accent of John F. Kennedy. Senator Jordan warned the convention of "the gap between the Negro middle-class politician and the Negro citizen. That citizen is beginning to hate us as much as he hates Whitey."

The question was whether any leaders who went to the black masses with anything less than a "Hate Whitey" program would have any chance of being heard. King's group has held back from the new apartheid policies of SNCC and CORE, and yet the old civil rights brotherhood theme is buried and the new theme was struck at the convention's "culture" night called "Black Is Beautiful; It's Beautiful to Be Black." It was like other such ethnic events in America in which, for instance, a Columbus Day crowd is harangued about the achievements of their distinguished countrymen, be they as devious as Machiavelli or as close at hand as the local Democratic district leader. A historic review of the achievements of the race at SCLC's conference night revealed that "black scientists" were responsible for such contributions to man's progress as the "invention of the machine gun," "the perfection of the blood plasma technique," and "the invention of the traffic light." A vocalist informed the audience before breaking into song that "nobody can sing blues but black people. Nobody can sing a gospel song but black people. Nobody in the whole world." When the lady had finished, with a song called "Time Is Winding Up . . . People Take Your Stand," the Reverend Andrew Young, a bright young lieutenant of the King forces, came to the microphone and said, "You know, hearing those songs, sung so beautifully, I felt like standing up and saying 'Black Power!'" He raised his right arm in the air as he intoned the magic words, and the audience erupted with cheering and applause.

In the new atmosphere of militancy in the nation's ghettos, merely "feeling like" saying black power did not seem enough to gain a real following. Hanging around outside the convention's sessions at the Ebenezer Baptist Church in Atlanta, I met a young Southern white man who said he had worked in the civil rights movement and had gone to jail in some of King's campaigns, but now he had seen the light, given up all civil rights activity, and enrolled in law school. He realized now that the old civil rights thing could never work, and that the black power groups were the only answer for the future. He said all white liberals were essentially "soft" and I asked what about the white college kids who had worked in the South, what about the ones who were killed in Mississippi during the "Freedom Summer," hadn't they proved they weren't soft? He smiled and said didn't I know those kids that were killed in Mississippi were a couple of Jewish boys and, "If they'd known there was any danger they'd have got out of town so fast you wouldn't have seen their dust."

So much for civil rights. The law student said he had come to the SCLC convention out of curiosity, but his suspicion had been confirmed that King was passé, not militant enough, and he cited the lack of many young people at the convention and the preponderance of middle-class, middle-age Negroes. He said things were moving fast, and the black power groups would be leading the way. He said he envied me because I was with the press and the press would get to see all the action of the coming revolution.

"There's going to be a lot of bloodshed," he said. "It really will be exhilarating."

D. *Formerly pacified elements of the society such as teachers, nurses, and even the Rockettes of Radio City catch the militant spirit in the land; a reporter wonders if they all have been eating fish or something*

The mood was obviously militant in the Adlai E. Stevenson Building, formerly the Temple Baptist Church, in Detroit. The great hall was almost packed to its capacity of five thousand, and it rocked with such old hymns of labor as "Solidarity Forever" and "The Union is Our Leader, We Shall Not Be Moved," sung with a gusto untypical of the current George Meany era of union establishmentarianism. The freshness of spirit, enthusiasm and excitement were not at all typical of what one associates with "labor" in the booming sixties, and in fact across town the boring drone of conventional union negotiations was going on between the United Auto Workers and the Ford Motor Company as both moved toward a strike that seemed like a stale ceremonial rite preceded by worn-out rhetoric from both sides and punctuated with frustrating press conferences in which reporters asked the ritual questions that of course could not be directly answered ("How long have you known *in your heart* there was going to be a strike, Mr. Reuther?"). But in the Stevenson Building there was a real passion in the proceedings, and genuine emotion in the crowd, which was quite middle-class in appearance, the men in business suits and ties and the

women in neat summer dresses. No, it did not look like a
labor crowd, nor did the signs of identification carried by
some of the delegations seem suited to the old-time labor
atmosphere—placards that said "Fitzgerald School" or "Park
Elementary." This was a meeting of the teachers of the
Detroit Public Schools, called by the Detroit Federation of
Teachers, but in tone and spirit it sounded more like a meeting of the United Mine Workers on the eve of some strike in
a tough Pennsylvania coal town in the heyday of John L.
Lewis.

Instead of a beetle-browed, deep-throated orator, however,
this meeting was chaired by a petite, reddish-haired lady
wearing glasses and a pretty, flowery dress and a homemade
badge that proudly said "Our Leader." The lady was Mary
Ellen Riordan ("The first name is a double name and I
insist on using both halves of it," she informed a visiting
reporter in no uncertain terms), President of the DFT, who
explained "Lord yes" she had been a teacher herself, she
taught science in the Detroit public schools and had since
1945. Miss Riordan seemed like the sort of teacher who
would be interesting and fair-minded but would tolerate no
nonsense; you would probably look forward to Miss Riordan's class but you would damn well know better than to
slouch in your seat or fiddle with the inkwell. Miss Riordan
and her union were opposed to just letting the government
appoint a panel to study their grievances; after all, she said,
that's what had happened with the police force and nothing
had ever come of it. A reporter pointed out that the panel
proposed to study the school situation had a thirty-day limit
on it, though, to which Miss Riordan said, "Isn't that nice."
As the crowd filed into the hall before the meeting began she
talked about these matters with me and several other press
people up on the platform and ended by assuring us with a
resounding slap on her notebook that "by *gosh* we're going

to have good schools!" and I for one did not doubt her for a
second.

The meeting had been called to urge the teachers to vote
that afternoon for a strike of the city's public schools, although Miss Riordan explained that "we are *not* going on a
strike—we are simply taking an extended summer recess. We
do not have a contract and we aren't going to work without a
contract." The idea of teachers "striking" has long been felt
to be improper if not immoral by much of the public, and
the attitude was long shared by the teachers themselves and
therefore a factor in their former pacification to generally
low salaries. Aside from the issue of children rather than
automobiles or refrigerators being affected by a teacher's
strike, there was the "class" sort of intimidation, the idea that
teachers were "professional people" and strikes were the sort
of thing indulged in by lower-class laboring sorts. Miss Riordan pointed out that "teachers were given the idea that being
a professional meant being a yes-man," and she noted that all
those years the teachers were maintaining their genteel "professional" image, "Blue-collar workers were making great
strides with the help of unions—they've come much farther
than we have. The wages of teachers and auto workers are
about the same now, but it takes us four years of college, and
twelve years of college work to get maximum pay." Most of
the other teachers obviously shared Miss Riordan's estimate
of the situation, and they overcame what for many must have
been real social qualms and went out on a real-live "strike,"
no matter what it was called for public relations purposes.
The union understood that this was all unfamiliar to its
members, and a bulletin listing twenty "Rules of Conduct
for the picket line" opened with the recognition that "for
most Detroit teachers, picketing will be a new experience,"
and offered reassurance that "Retail Workers' Hall will be
open from 2:00 to 7:00 P.M. for vote tabulation, picket sign

materials, morale pills, group therapy, coffee and companionship." From the sound of the meeting, it seemed as if they had already taken their "morale pills."

The teachers in Detroit stayed out picketing for thirteen days and won an across-the-board raise of $1,700 over two years, reduction in the school year from forty to thirty-nine weeks, and a limitation of class size to thirty-nine pupils. The city and state had argued that the money to meet the teachers' demands was not available, but "by gosh" it somehow *became* available.

And the teachers in Detroit were not an isolated case. There were strikes of teachers throughout the state of Michigan, in New York City, Fort Lauderdale, Florida, East St. Louis, and Paducah, Kentucky. The militance spread as these middle-class professional people took to the picket lines, many for the first time in their lives. Nor was it only teachers, but also nurses in a number of cities, and even that All-American chorus line, the high kickers of Radio City Music Hall, bastion of middle-class American entertainment. Instead of precision-kicking on the mammoth stage with the traditional fixed grins and the scanty costumes designed for the latest "extravaganza," there were the famed Rockettes in rain and wind hoofing it on the sidewalks of New York with signs like one that succinctly told the story of the bearer's oppressive situation: "I'm a Rockette. I get $4.12 a show and rehearse forty hours for nothing."

Nothing seemed sacred anymore; the bakers of Mom's apple pies might even be next to strike.

✦ ✦ ✦

FIREMEN
WALK OUT
IN SAGINAW

SAGINAW — Thirty-eight firemen who comprise the afternoon shift of Saginaw's 100-man fire department

locked the fire station doors and walked
off their jobs Tuesday night because
of a pay dispute with the city.

"We've got a crisis on our hands,"
Edward Potthoff, City Manager, said.
He declined further comment.

— the *Detroit* Free Press, *September
6, 1967*

❖   ❖   ❖

A couple of days after the Detroit teachers started walking
their picket lines, I went over to DFT headquarters with
Harry Bernstein, labor editor of the Los Angeles *Times*, to
try to learn a little more about the new militancy of the
teachers from Miss Riordan. She was on her way to visit some
of the troops, but stopped long enough to chat with us. Bernstein was curious, as I was, about the seemingly overnight
mood of militancy that had possessed the teachers.

"There's a real social revolution sweeping the teaching
profession," Miss Riordan said. "It's being felt all over the
country. Teachers are increasingly becoming aware of their
own value and their scarcity and taking a hard look at where
they can best use their talents."

"But why *now*, all of a sudden?" Bernstein asked. "Have
you all been eating fish or something?"

Miss Riordan smiled and said that she didn't know of
anything like that, but, "We're finally getting through. For
one thing there's an increasing number who are in it as a
career and not just a hobby."

But that couldn't explain it all either; Bernstein wondered
if the increasing example of Negro militancy might have
anything to do with it and Miss Riordan agreed that maybe
that was part of it, too.

Beyond these "parts" there was no way of pinning it down,
any more than there was of explaining the militancy in other

groups and professions throughout the country except that the whole mood must surely be feeding back and forth in all these different areas, people seeing one race or class or profession demanding better things and thinking, why not me, too, why shouldn't I get a bigger share of this enormous, rich pie that the country is producing?

As for more specific explanations, until it is disproved by in-depth studies of blue-ribbon commissions and interdisciplinary research teams, I tend to go with the Harry Bernstein Theory of Social Militancy in Advanced Societies: maybe everyone's been eating a lot of fish or something.

E. *There is believed to be a revolution in culture and the arts; seeing is believing*

One hears and reads a great deal about revolutionary movements and upheavals in the creative arts in the country. In every field, whatever tradition there was has become unfashionable, and most new works are judged on the issue of whether or not they represent a "breakthrough" in their particular area.

Especially among the young and the cognoscenti (who attempt to keep their own reactions in step with the young), "the film" is the principal new art form. It is generally felt that, as one collegian expressed it, the film has replaced the novel as the main form of creative expression for his generation.

In many ways this fits in with other prevailing trends in the culture. There is movement, excitement, and overall distraction in going out with a camera and taking pictures of people. It is much more entertaining than sitting alone in a room and grinding out words. Also, it is more convivial, and the novice film maker is more likely to meet pretty girls in the course of his work than if he were shut up in some garret with pen and paper. In Harvard Square, in Cambridge, Mass., many young men roam around with cameras, and often are able to make the acquaintance of a young lady by asking if she would like to be in a film he is making—or is about to make. The offer is flattering, and, in the name of art, can hardly be refused. I met one young girl who was quite excited because she had just been asked by a young

man in the Square to be in a film he was making. She was to
be at his apartment the next evening at 9 P.M. for the first
shooting. I asked her what kind of film it was going to be,
and she said "an underground film." I asked if she knew
what the film was going to be about. She said the only thing
she knew about it was the title. I asked her what it was, and
she said, "Desire."

It is rumored that many of the cameras the young men
carry do not have any film in them.

While in Hollywood I talked with Dalton Trumbo, who is
one of the finest scriptwriters of America, and has won a
number of Academy Awards, some of them under other
names during the time when he was living in exile in Mexico
because of being blacklisted during the great internal anti-
Communist days of the fifties. Trumbo of course would be
regarded as a "movie" writer rather than a "film" writer.
Many films do not need writers at all. Trumbo is a lively,
energetic little man who has a white moustache and smokes
cigars and talks very quickly and intensely about almost
everything, and is altogether too enthusiastic to ever make it
as a culture hero in the cool new world of "film."

I was interested in what he thought about some of the new
"breakthroughs" in film, and I asked if he had seen *Blow-
Up,* directed by an Italian film prince and produced and cast
in England. *Blow-Up* has split film lovers into warring
camps of controversy, but most all agree that it made a number of breakthroughs, and so it was of the first order of importance. It concerns (though is not "about") a photogra-
pher who witnesses a murder and has other meaningful and
symbolic adventures before and after, which are open to a
wide range of interpretation. In fact, the central event of the
movie is open to interpretation, since part of the film lovers'
arguments rage around the question whether or not the
murder really happened at all. In classic "tragedy" it would

be quite a handicap if the audience didn't know whether a person who was murdered was really murdered. But Tragedy has for some time been out of style and Illusion has replaced it. To foster the sense of Illusion, *Blow-Up* begins with a mime troupe cavorting through the streets and the mime troupe is not seen again until the end of the film, when they play an imaginary tennis game without any equipment.

Trumbo had indeed seen this film and he puffed rapidly on his cigar when I asked him about it, and said, "Well, it was technically exciting, but a lot of those technical things have been done a long time ago. I was talking with Katie Hepburn the other day, and she happened to have seen *Blow-Up* recently, and I rather liked her reaction to it. 'You know,' she said, 'Spencer and I used to do that sort of thing, only we used real tennis balls.' "

✦ ✦ ✦

THE ART WORLD
The Nineteen-Sixties:
Time in the Museum

It is precisely the collective thinking represented in "The Sixties" [an exhibition at the Museum of Modern Art] that makes it (and its exclusions) significant as a reflection of current trends in the public life of art. Between the 1959 junk sculpture of Richard Stankiewicz or the 1960 kitchen-litter assemblage of Daniel Spoerri and the glass-and-chromium cube of Larry Bell or the painted-aluminum sections of Ronald Bladen, drastic changes have taken place in the selection of materials, as well as in prevalent feeling, attitudes, and ideas. Most obviously, painting has been steadily deemphasized . . .

— *Harold Rosenberg, the* New Yorker

✦ ✦ ✦

Although there are a number of quite excellent writers of novels and poems who continue doing their work, the public hears little or nothing about them. They are not making breakthroughs, nor are they public personalities in jet-set social circles. This may seem irrelevant, but it is extremely important in the cultural life of supernation. The overall situation in this area can best be explained by an observation made by Gay Talese in *Esquire* magazine, which seems to me to make further comment unnecessary: "One must be *seen* to exist, for now there is no other proof. There is no longer an identity in craft, only in self-promotion. There are no acts, only scenes."

F. *A Sexual Revolution is said to have freed the populace from guilt and frustration; the Sexual Freedom League of Oakland discusses its program at an open meeting; venereal disease on rise in Indianapolis*

From reading the nation's magazines, I learned that a Sexual Revolution in the society had dispelled the former guilts and fears concerning sex that once were quite common in a nation with deep Puritan traditions. The sexual revolution has been written about for some time, and it is now usually referred to as an accomplished fact, one of the great changes that has come to pass and now is accepted by everyone whether they like it or not, just like social security or welfare or universal suffrage, one of the great advances made by a free society.

Perhaps the most militant organization concerned with this revolution is the Sexual Freedom League, whose statement of position explains: "We believe that sexual expression, in whatever form agreed upon between consenting persons of either sex, should be considered an inalienable human right." The League seems to be strongest in California, where most of the more advanced social movements have their greatest strength, and while in that sunny state I noticed in one of the underground papers an announcement of a meeting of the Oakland League for Sexual Freedom which was open to the public. This seemed to afford an excellent opportunity for finding what, if anything, remained to be accomplished in the sexual revolution, and how its most militant adherents were engaged in bringing about the last stages of emancipation.

I arrived about fifteen minutes late and had some difficulty pushing my way into the crowded meeting. The League's Oakland headquarters consist of a medium-sized room above a beauty shop and the crowd had spilled over into the hallway. I managed to shove my way inside, however, and found a seat on the floor. The first thing that struck me was the audience itself, which was largely middle-aged and middle-class in appearance, and also overwhelmingly male. According to the best count I could make, there were seventy-three men and eleven women. As I learned later, most of the women were wives who had been brought by their husbands.

Everyone was listening attentively to a pleasant-looking man about thirty years old, casually dressed in an open-necked sport shirt and slacks. He was talking about the fact that masturbation was "not really harmful," and I wondered if that particular subject was considered to be one of the burning issues facing the vanguard of the sexual revolution. There did not, at any rate, seem to be any open controversy over that bold statement, and the man went on to explain some of the different activities of the group. The "committees" of people interested in a particular area of the revolution were referred to as "circles," a term commonly used by church organizations to describe their subgroups, such as the Sewing Circle, etc. The Oakland SFL offered to prospective members a "sketching circle," where nude models were used, an "outdoor circle" for nude beach activities, and a "legal action circle" which picketed for legalization of abortion and other issues of sexual freedom. The man who seemed to be the chairman explained a little about some of these and similar "circles" and a well-dressed, intelligent-looking young man in the audience raised his hand and said: "I've never been to one of your meetings before, but I sort of assumed that as well as these different circles you've mentioned, that, well, since it *is* the Sexual Freedom League, well, I mean, isn't there just a circle where men and women get together who like to have sex with each other?"

There was an embarrassed silence, and then the chairman said, "Oh, you mean—well, something like a 'screwing circle.' "

There was nervous laughter, but the young man boldly confirmed that that was pretty much what he meant.

The chairman explained that the problem was, in their experience, when they held an "open" party like that they only got about two or three women to attend, and fifty to a hundred men.

A chubby blonde lady sitting on the floor near the front turned to the newcomer and explained further that when you have single men and women come to such a party "you get a lot of weirdos."

The chairman vouched for that, and said you even got some weirdos who came to parties where only couples were allowed; there was one such "perverse" sort of person who went around at such a party turning lights on while people were in intimate situations! A man who looked around ninety years old asked where was one of those nude beaches he had heard about. A younger man in the audience complained he had been to a nude beach and there weren't any women at all but all these other men were looking at him with great interest and he said, "They made me feel like *I* was the girl."

The chairman said sometimes the League planned outings

to such beaches, but he reminded the group that some families brought their children and so there should be "no hanky-panky" on those occasions.

The chairman said that refreshments would be served, and so everyone stood up and crowded around a little table at the front which had paper cups, coffee, and two gallon bottles of California red wine. I went over and introduced myself to the fellow who had asked the question about the "screwing circle," and told him I felt he had made a valid point. He turned out to be an assistant district attorney in a large city in the East, was a bachelor, and had come out to California for his vacation because of the "swinging scene" he had heard about in San Francisco and the Bay area. He said he liked the hippie girls he had seen, many of whom "walk around with these short skirts and don't have any underwear on." He had not, however, made the acquaintance of any of those girls—or indeed of any girls at all.

A middle-aged lady came over and asked if we were visiting the League for the first time and we said we were. She said she and her husband were members of the sketching circle, and found it quite enjoyable. The Assistant D.A. asked if he might come to one of their meetings, and the lady looked somewhat shocked and pointed to a poster describing the circle's activities which said that participants must have "real talent" for art.

"We only allow couples," the lady explained. "We found that sometimes single men came and didn't really sketch at all, but just looked at the model in a—well, in a disturbing way."

I suggested to the Assistant D.A. that we go somewhere and have a drink. He agreed that would be a good idea, and we pushed our way toward the door. On the way out, I stopped and looked at a large homemade poster that seemed to illustrate the principles of the League for Sexual Freedom.

114 SUPERNATION AT PEACE AND WAR

There were a lot of little "hearts" floating around a large heart, and in the little hearts were words like "honesty" and "self-enlightenment," and in the big heart was the word "LOVE." There seemed to me no reason at all why the League could not widen its membership by gaining endorsements from responsible public figures. I could detect nothing in its poster of principles, or in fact in the discussion of the meeting, that could not be endorsed by the Reverend Billy Graham, Richard Nixon, or even George Romney, to name but a few of the nation's leading moralists.

✦ ✦ ✦

Shy, would-be Romeos seeking compatible girls to teach us what it's all about. (If you already wrote and your letter was returned by mistake by the PO please write again) Box 1487, GPO, NY, NY 10001.

— *personal ad in the* East Village Other, *an underground newspaper in New York City*

On the verge of suicide. Only hope is good Christian man who wants me and will take care of me. Have mental illness but with good man would make it on my proper medicine. Man who is very humble and kind and believes all people & demons will be saved and who wants to live as brother & sister ONLY please come out to see me. This is not a phony ad. Husband is divorcing me for another & I can't support myself. Men like this 30-45 please come out and help me. Please no phonies. Terese, 11909 Ramona Ave., Hawthorne, Calif. (house in rear).

— *personal ad in the Los Angeles Free Press, an underground newspaper*

✦ ✦ ✦

The Assistant D.A. had rented a car for his swinging summer vacation, and we drove in to San Francisco from the SFL meeting in Oakland. He asked if I had yet taken in any of the "topless" places which had become such a rage and I said no, but I certainly felt my researches would not be complete without doing so. There were so many different topless shows that it was difficult to know which to choose; the "topless" art form had become so commonplace that any new wrinkles were sought to attract customers, such as the show whose featured performer was billed as the "Topless Mother of Eight Children!"

More interested in the classic stage of the art than in the rococo phase, we rejected the topless mother of eight and decided to take in the performance of Miss Carol Doda, described as the *original* topless dancer of San Francisco. We were seated at a small table among many others, and then the lights went out and an MC came to a microphone under a single spot and said, "You've read about her in *Playboy, Esquire, Life,* and *Cavalier* . . . now here she is, Carol Doda!" The band struck up, and all eyes were raised upward, as Miss Doda made her entrance by descending from what looked like a fur-lined manhole in the ceiling. She was a blonde, wearing something like the bottom part of a bikini, and high heels. She moved in time to the music, her large breasts bobbing up and down. Then she and the platform she stood on were raised up again through the fur-lined manhole and disappeared. The lights came on. The show was over. We had witnessed yet another of the daring advances in the sexual revolution.

❖　❖　❖

V.D. CURB GAINS
AGENCY SUPPORT
By Rick Johnson

Dr. Henry G. Nester, City Council health director, yesterday pledged his support to a proposed new health code

designed to protect the public from
venereal disease and smash a $5.8-mil-
lion-a-year prostitution racket in Indianapolis.
      . . . State Board of Health statistics
released earlier this year showed that
Indianapolis had a higher ratio of reported cases of venereal disease than
Los Angeles and Miami combined and
25 percent more than New York City.
      But according to Dr. Albert Marshall,
director of the State Health Board's
division of communicable diseases, and
the American Social Health Association,
only one of every four cases of venereal
disease is reported.
      — the Indianapolis Star, September
15, 1967

✦　✦　✦

It would seem that some of the claims of the sexual revolution have been exaggerated. More men seem to be interested
in the new sexual freedoms than women, a factor which even
operates among the young generation of "free-spirited" kids,
including hippies. Robert Scheer, an editor of *Ramparts*
magazine who lives in San Francisco and is well acquainted
with its various scenes, pointed out a quite significant cir-
cumstance which is rarely mentioned in the glamorous reports about Haight-Ashbury. "The ratio of men to women is
about ten to one," he estimated. "For that reason alone, it
has to be a pretty unhappy scene." This male-heavy ratio has
also been noted in some of the underground papers, and
naturally, lamented. The famous "personal" advertisements
of those papers are overwhelmingly ones in which men are
seeking women. Picking an issue of the underground press at
random, I counted in the personal ads of one issue of the
East Village Other twenty ads placed by men seeking women,
one ad of a man seeking a man, and one of a woman seeking
a man (the woman specified in her ad that she was looking

only for men "who want a girlfriend, not a pickup"). This was a typical ratio.

In movies, bookstores, television, "topless" bars, and magazines, the society seems flooded with every kind of sexual goody, available to all. But most of this display of erotica is display only; it is for looking at rather than possessing, like the bunnies at the Playboy Club, whom the customer can look at, even talk with, but mustn't touch. The average customer in the great American sex market pays not for flesh but for fantasy, indeed a revolutionary change from the older, pre-emancipated European tradition.

Beyond the Bunny-type glitter there of course are real girls next door, and no doubt more of them engage in sexual intercourse in and out of marriage than did their older sisters of a generation back. There are all the new contraceptive devices, led by the fabulous "pill," which supposedly have dispelled all of women's fears. But if the majority of them feel free about employing these contraceptive measures, why is abortion still one of the great issues of the day? Why do so many of these women, many of them middle-class and many of them married, become pregnant when they do not intend or wish to be, and when they have all the modern varieties of contraception available to them?

Does guilt still make the pill a bitter one to swallow? Is pill taking secretly felt to represent premeditated, and therefore nonspontaneous, and therefore non-love-inspired (and therefore evil) sexual activity? That would be an interesting line of questioning for someone to pursue in a study of the real extent and meaning of the sexual revolution. Suggested supplementary reading might well include the collected sermons of Cotton Mather.

G. Militant leaders of the feminine revolution want freedom NOW; separation of the sexes may be the final solution

> With the rise of the peasant movement, the women in many places have begun to organize rural women's associations; the opportunity has come for them to lift up their heads, and the authority of the husband is getting shakier every day. . . .
>
> —*Quotations from Chairman Mao Tse-tung*

The Feminine Revolution should not be confused with the Sexual Revolution. The feminine revolution seeks to obliterate the distinctions between male and female, thus making them both "equal." This goal, if fully achieved, would certainly cut the ground out from under the sexual revolution.

The feminine revolution has made great strides, particularly among college-educated women. Especially in some of the leading women's colleges, the students are made to feel that if they do not choose a career and become successful in their field after graduation, they are failures. In one such college (probably in many) the girls are told upon entering that they are "special" in having been accepted there, and that if they merely get married and settle down and raise a family after graduation they will have "betrayed" their education as well as the institution in which they were so fortunate to receive it.

In pre-feminine-revolutionary days, there were some women who did not enjoy the life of a housewife and mother, and yet because of the social climate they were likely to feel guilty and unnatural if they wished to pursue a career. Now, among most college-trained women, there are some who do not enjoy the life of a career, and yet because of the social climate they are likely to feel guilty and unnatural if they wish to pursue the life of a wife and mother.

The extremely complex and demanding job of being successful in the roles of wife and mother, a job which requires the most creative command and application of psychological, economic, sexual, and managerial skills, is no longer considered a "job" at all, much less a career, but simply a form of servitude. The woman who pursues it is regarded by the society at large as "just a housewife," for which it is deemed necessary to apologize.

Like many a minority revolt in a certain stage of ferment, the feminine revolution has recently taken on a political nature, and is attempting to press its advance through action at the polls. The most militant organization in this revolution is the National Organization for Women (NOW), which at its last annual convention served warning on elected officials everywhere by urging its followers to "cross party lines to elect candidates who support equality for women, and to defeat its enemies."

Betty Friedan, who is author of *The Feminine Mystique,* the females' "Communist Manifesto," is appropriately enough the President of NOW, and at the group's convention she attacked President Johnson for making only "token appointments" for women in top government positions.

In the political sense, it is obvious that the Negroes are ahead of the women in their revolution, for there are no women on the Supreme Court, there is no U.S. Commission on Women's Rights, and most politicians don't even bother to make a special effort to solicit the female vote.

The fact that the women are now complaining about "tokenism" indicates that they are lagging about five to eight years behind the Negro revolution. If they follow the stages of the Negro minority in its own struggle for equal rights, it may be that in a decade or even less the militant women's organizations will have scorned the male population altogether and become primarily concerned with "Female Power." The most radical of their leaders will advocate complete separation of the sexes, arguing that living together was tried and never worked because males always secretly regarded them as inferior, an attitude ingrained by the many years in which the male population held them in slavery. Those women who still feel some accommodation can be made with the men will be scorned as "Aunt Jemimas." There may be an attempt at some sort of political coalition with the militant females and the most liberal males (those who will do anything to please them) but if such a coalition convention is held the women will demand more votes than the men, some of the men will walk out of the convention in a huff, and the militant women will say gleefully that it only proved that those men who left never understood the true aspirations of their revolution anyway.

It is doubtful that even Betty Friedan knows where it will end. Perhaps she should consult Stokely Carmichael.

H. *"Wanted, dead or alive: God"; religion hit by drop-out problem; hippies scorn a hymn-in*

> Their religion itself is based on the notion that a vague, undefined and diffused supernatural power floods the universe. This power may manifest itself through mankind, through animate and inanimate objects, as well as natural phenomenon. This power has no intrinsic qualities of good or evil. The virtue of this power is its potency. . . .
>
> The philosophical premises are . . . that the universe is full of danger, and that human relationships are based on kinship.

This belief was developed and practiced on the North American continent by the aboriginal Indian tribes. It was, however, considered primitive by the Europeans who settled and civilized the continent. In contrast to the simple and superstitious religion of the natives as outlined in the above summary, the new settlers brought a more sophisticated theological system, built around the concept of an all-powerful God whose only begotten son was conceived in a Virgin birth in a remote part of Asia, announced himself as the savior of all mankind, and preached the doctrines of his father until the age of thirty-three, when he was nailed to a cross until dead, but three days later rose from the dead, promising eternal life to all men, and ascended to Heaven (the paradise which good Christians achieve after death) and took his place at the right hand of God, his Father.

This more advanced Christian doctrine was taught to all

the native Indians who were not eradicated in the westward spread of the white Europeans' civilization across the continent. Most of the native Indians who survived the onrush of civilization were placed on "reservations," where many still remain and some still adhere to the old beliefs of their fathers in spite of the constant help given them by their conquerers, as illustrated by the work of the young scholar who wrote the brief quoted description of Indian religion in a paper entitled: "Insights Into Some Influencing Factors in the Reservation Indians' Environment and Their Relevance to the Cross-Ethnic Counselor."

The advanced and sophisticated religious concepts embodied by Christianity became the predominant faith of the nation and still remain so, but in recent years a troubling wave of doubt and controversy has shaken that faith. Certain of its own leading theologians have publicly announced that "God," presumably the all-powerful God worshipped in their own religion, has "died." The alleged "Death of God" has stirred great controversy in the land, resulting in charges and countercharges concerning such formerly undisputed questions as the death, survival, relevance, health, and even popularity of "God" Himself. The claim of God's death was first made by a Protestant professor of theology in the unlikely (because supposedly firm in faith) southern city of Atlanta, Georgia. The obituary was refuted by many but ignored by few, and no stronghold of the faith was immune from the dispute. An article was published in the *Alumnus* magazine of Notre Dame University, a Catholic institution, with the provocative title: "Wanted Dead or Alive: God." Nor was the debate limited to clerical circles. In the city of Indianapolis a large sign at an intersection of heavy traffic urged citizens to "Teach 4th and 5th Graders God is Alive— Support Religious Education," a message made public

by "Courtesy Independence Insurance Agents of Indianapolis, Inc."

The controversy must surely be in part responsible for the
fact that God, like the nation's President, has slumped in the
all-important opinion polls of the country. Though God has
not yet been subjected to specific issues of public opinion as
has the President, such as whether or not the citizen feels
that He has been "doing a good job" in the performance of
his office, nevertheless, His overall popularity has been measured and found to be falling. The Gallup Poll, which pro-
nounces itself able to measure religious as well as political
trends, found that in 1967, 57 percent of adult Americans
felt that the influence of religion was in decline, whereas ten
years before, the same polling agency had discovered that 59
percent of the populace felt that the influence of religion was
growing. Attendance at church services had dropped in that
period, from 49 percent to 44 percent of the adult population, and the decline of worship attendance among young
people of the 19-to-21-year-old age category was twice as high
as the national average. The situation was put most bluntly
by the Reverend Dr. Eugene Carson Blake, head of the
World Council of Churches (representing more than 300
million Christians of Protestant, Anglican, and Orthodox
denominations), when he told a meeting of his council last
year that "God is strictly nonsense in the popular mind
today."

Not only laymen but clergy were dropping out of the ranks
of the church. Catholic priests were revolting against their
vows in order to marry, at the rate of about one thousand a
year, and one expert said that priests were leaving their voca-
tion because of reasons that included "loss of faith" and "loss
of chastity." According to *Atlanta* magazine, in a single
month during the past year, a local executive was "asked to

help three of the city's outstanding young clergymen find jobs outside the church." The situation was not unique, the article claimed, noting that seminary enrollments had dropped steadily in the past decade, and of 17,000 seminary students recently queried, only a third said they planned to stay in the ministry.

All this should not be taken to indicate that the defection has gone so far as to undermine the basic religious commitments of the nation. One of the reasons for the nation's very founding was the principle of "religious freedom," the freedom of men to worship whatever way they chose, and if this principle did not seem to be applied to the native inhabitants of the land, who were sent missionaries on the reservations where they were contained, it has allowed the Jews, the Mormons, the Moslems, and any other religious sect to practice its beliefs. But while *tolerating* this diversion, the nation has held firm to the Christian faith, as exemplified by its principal holidays (the most significant being the celebration of the Virgin birth of Jesus Christ, the son of God). The description of the United States as a "Christian Nation" would still seem to be valid, as witnessed for example at Arlington Cemetery in a Veterans Day ceremony, which ended with a benediction by the Reverend Harold B. Fay, National Chaplain of Veterans of World War I, who asked God to bless the nation "until the end of time" and added that this request was made "In the name of thy son and our savior, Jesus Christ our Lord," which if it did not eliminate would seem to minimize any requests of those veterans present of Jewish or any other non-Christian faith.

Despite the national alliance with the God of the Christian religion, which did not seem in any danger of dissolution, the defection and disillusionment of lay and clergy elements in the society were perhaps a main reason for the popularity, the fashionability, and the hopeful goodwill engendered in some sections of the population toward the hippie movement. In its talk of Love, its rejection of material values, it made many middle-aged people as well as young men and women share the feeling of Mrs. Dagmar Wilson, an intelligent leader of the women's peace movement, that the young hippies represented "a style and an ethic that made her think of early Christianity," according to one of her interviewers.

Indeed there is much ritual in the hippie culture, and I thought about its religious aspects when I went to a Sunday fest that the Diggers held in a small park near Haight-Ashbury one gray and soggy Sunday afternoon. While approaching I saw a group of people dancing gaily on a small hill around some others who were singing. The singers turned out to be clean-shaven and modestly dressed, while those who danced around them wore hippie garb. The singers were singing old-fashioned and unfashionable religious hymns, and the hippies were taunting them. Down below, a rock 'n' roll group was bleating and a bearded hippie stopped the hymn singers in mid-hymn and asked if they would make a donation to the cost of the loudspeaker for the rock group. The hymn singers remained unperturbed but declined to contribute, and a gray-haired lady who seemed to be their leader explained they had brought no money. The bearded hippie began yelling to the assembled of his own faith, "See, that's their religion, that's where it's at. Fuck it!" The hymn singers struck up again, one of them playing the accordion. There were seven of them standing on the hill, five older men and women, one pale and very beautiful young girl, and a tall young man who spoke of how God had saved him while the others hummed in the background. These people turned out to be the Voice of Pentecost Singers from the United Pentacostal Church of 21st and Capp Street in San Francisco. The Pentacostal faith is very unfashionable and yet has made great conversions among the poor of the big cities, among unfashionable people who give up drinking and smoking, and former narcotics addicts who even give up drugs in their conversion. The Pentacostals smiled and sang through the taunts and ridicule of the hippies, and then they walked off together down the hill. I went up and thanked them and said their singing was very fine, and the young man brightened and handed me a mimeographed leaflet. When I got back to my hotel I read it, and inside was a short essay from which I present here some key excerpts.

The Long Lonely Search

Each of we humans differ in appearance as well as in taste, this makes us different from any of the other world's animals.

Each seek and reach out because of one need or another, each of us have passions, each of us has hunger, these most usually are for love, knowledge, and to know mankind, either in pity or revulgence.

. . . To fill the void, the horrible abyss, that at one time or another faces all, in the forms of loneliness, despair, humiliation, man needs fellowship. This fellowship—when promulgated in Christian ethics and warp, kindred with belief and compassion makes again a world in which the lost may live, and the spurned may find love. . . .

Last, and beautiful be it, to love again, our God and fellow man. . . .

The message no doubt would be judged theologically simple. In fact, in its spirit, it sort of reminded me of the Indians.

II

Pacification of the home front poses special problems in a democracy, but many powerful forces work for such conditions; "silence" is found not only in the center of society, but also on some of the fringes

According to my Webster's dictionary the verb "to pacify" means to quell or calm. The word has become popular in recent years owing to its usage in the war in Vietnam, where U.S. and South Vietnamese government troops do not "conquer" villages which are sympathetic to the enemy, but "pacify" them. The "pacification" is effected not only by force and the threat of force but also by persuasion, indoctrination, and reward in the form of soap, candy, and medical supplies and services (actual military instructions for this type of pacification will be described later).

It is obviously the job of any government to "quell or calm" its own populace as well as its enemies, and in some countries this is done by force alone, which is probably the simplest method. That is not the way things are done in a democracy, however, except as a last resort (as in the quelling of lawless revolts or riots in the streets by government troops and armor). The basic philosophy of the American system is perhaps best explained by the document called "Channeling," issued by the U.S. Selective Service System in 1965. Though referring to the draft, the principles apply to other domestic areas as well:

> The psychology of granting wide choice under pressure to take action is the American or indirect way of achieving what is done by direction in foreign countries where choice is not permitted. Here, choice is limited but not denied, and it is fundamental that an individual generally applies himself better to something he has decided to do rather than something he has been told to do.

There of course are different methods of quelling and calming, some more effective than others, some more controversial than others. One approach to pacification is symbolized by what is known as "a pacifier," the nipple-shaped rubber device that is placed in the mouth of a baby to keep it from crying. In social terms this concept has a negative connotation, as expressed by the Reverend Hosea Williams at the SCLC convention when he said the government's poverty program was only a "sugar teat" to keep the poor people quiet.

Many middle-class citizens were shocked and offended when it seemed to them that this type of minimal aid to the poor resulted evidently not in their pacification but in their revolt; when instead of being grateful for what they were given, these people cried for more. And yet it is most often found that people who have nothing and are taught to expect nothing are less likely to rebel than people who have a little bit and are taught to expect a lot. In this sense it is a dangerous and courageous act for the government to initiate such a raising up of the oppressed in any manner at all, and when the first stirrings of revolt occur, the government is then pushed by forces from two opposing sides: those who wish to give the underprivileged people nothing, which in fact helps "keep them in their place" (at the bottom), and those who wish to raise them immediately to the average level of abundance of the society.

The fears and unrest aroused by these social contradictions and changes are more difficult to pacify than the disturbances aroused by the "limited war" in Vietnam, for they are more relevant to the immediate lives of more people, and having been unleashed they hold less promise of being "negotiated" out of existence.

But one of the major factors for pacification of uneasiness about the war abroad and the war in the streets of the nation is that both are largely "invisible" to the majority. Michael Harrington in his book on the nation's poor, *The Other America,* noted that the poor were largely "invisible" because they were mostly off in their own segregated ghettos, not often passed through or seen by the middle-class affluent Americans.

In a different sense the war in Vietnam is also "ghettoized," for it is "limited" not only abroad but at home. Patriotic demonstrations in support of the war have come as the result of private individuals and groups rather than government initiation. There are no parades of returning veterans, no call for a home-front effort such as there was in World War II to collect scrap metal, tinfoil, and paper for the "war effort," no special drive for what used to be called War Bonds before the nation gave up War and adopted Defense, no Victory gardens to raise small patches of carrots or tomatoes that would somehow help defeat the enemy, no rationing of essential goods or services. All this is not by accident. The President has privately said that the government's reluctance about initiating such a wartime atmosphere is part of its responsibility, part of the policy of "restraint." He has explained that to stir such sentiment would be simple, and yet dangerous, for it would unleash the sort of superpatriotism that would call for greater escalation and for greater intolerance toward dissent. And yet there is in the administration's boast of restraint an implied threat—the sense that the restraint is a favor it is doing the country, and that if the citizens do not behave well, the government will have to use less restraint in dealing with the home front, will have to stoke up the patriotism a little more and crack down on dissenters who seem to be having a real effect, the sort of crackdown represented by the indictments of Dr. Spock and the other four adults for urging draft resistance.

There is another side to the government's restraining itself from promoting superpatriotism. For if it is sacrificing support it could gain for itself by such restraint, it is also limiting the potential of more widespread opposition to the war. The main effect of the war on most people, whether they think of it consciously or not, has been prosperity at home, and an increase of more than a million jobs in the two-year period ending in September of 1967. So, except for the young who go to war and their families, most people are not directly touched by it, and as "news" it is only part of the vast outpouring of action and conflict and controversy all over the nation and the world. In the midst of their own problems with job and home and neighbors, with a million personal details and diversions, most men are unlikely to "take a stand" about an issue which does not bear on them directly and which is not an everyday part of their consciousness.

In spite of the diversity of dissent discussed earlier, in spite of the serious nature of some of the domestic revolutions, the mass of the society proceeds with its daily routine. Most men obey authority, accept direction from above, and are loyal to their country as a matter of instinctive response. The most successful sort of pacification is not military or legal enforcement by the government, but the "natural" calming influences which are built into the society, and which in a sense the people provide for themselves.

A. *It is observed that people help provide for their own pacification through watching and participating in rituals such as sports and social life*

---

i. *The government worries about citizens seeing the war on television, but more watch the ball game anyway; a six-pack in the refrigerator helps to quell and calm the modern man*

There are probably more things to demand a man's attention in supernation than in any other society in history, and this helps keep the pacification. The communications media are of course a great source of distraction as well as information, and they have great potential for rousing as well as pacifying the populace. That is why totalitarian governments exercise full control of the press and the airwaves. In a democracy, however, censorship is not favored except in time of total war, and the "American, or indirect, way" of influence is used. The government can "manage the news" in the sense of releasing or withholding what it wishes, and in presenting information in the language and manner most likely to gain public support.

Fearing the political repercussions of imposing wartime censorship, the government has tried "indirectly" to affect the press, but this is often frustrating, as in the case of President Kennedy's unsuccessful request that the New York *Times* withdraw David Halberstam, Saigon correspondent who was writing critical dispatches of the war in its early phases. The government would prefer that the press impose its own censorship, a view most vividly expressed by White House Press Secretary George Christian, who recently exploded about a critical news dispatch from Saigon. When asked by a correspondent if the report was accurate, Christian explained, "I don't care if it's right or wrong. Even if you have it nailed down—laid out cold in your lap—you don't write that kind of story."

The administration seems to be even more worried about television than about the press, not so much for what it says as for what it shows about the war. Every administration official I talked with said that the main reason for the widespread domestic opposition to the war was that, as one of them put it. "people are able to see it live on television, they see people getting killed right in their living room." Last year after a news film of American soldiers setting fire to a Vietnamese village was shown on TV, the President summoned network officials to Washington and lectured them on their "responsibilities." Erwin Knoll, Washington correspondent of Newhouse newspapers, said that while some people felt this effected a change in TV war coverage, it was "not nearly as great a change as the administration wished."

The administration's feelings on the matter were probably best expressed when the White House invited some correspondents to hear the opinion of Walter Judd, a conservative Republican and staunch war supporter who had just returned from Vietnam. The reporters met with Dr. Judd in George Christian's office, and Judd told them:

"I think we have to reexamine whether it is possible for a free people to carry on a prolonged struggle on a peacetime basis, especially with the new means of communication, like the television. There are cruelties in every war. Men have known them. There have been accidents with civilians. . . . These things happen. . . . But the wives and children didn't see them on television at six o'clock at night."

✦ ✦ ✦

COMBAT

In an advertisement for a TV program called Combat, two American GI's in World War II garb were looking out at a blasted village.

Sgt.: We have to take that house.
Pvt.: We can't take that house without a tank.
Sgt.: We have to.
Pvt.: Why?
Sgt.: We were told to.
Explosions, then fadeout.
A voice says that "combat separates the men from the boys, the quick from the dead."

✦ ✦ ✦

In the course of my own travels through the country, I never met anyone who had come to oppose the war because of having seen it "live" on television. Of course it is possible that such influence is subconscious, and the citizen may have unknowingly come to oppose the war because of such an experience. My own feeling, however, is that a more realistic analysis of the influence of television on the public was made by some TV cameramen in the White House Press lobby. The photographers were bemoaning the fact that they were going to have to cover the antiwar demonstrations at the Pentagon scheduled for the coming Saturday. It was argued and agreed that the networks were crazy to think that the general public was interested in such stuff, and in fact most viewers would surely get mad if the afternoon's college football game of the week were in any way interrupted by such nonsense.

"Imagine," said one of the photographers, "a guy has just settled down in front of his TV set, he's taken off his shoes, he has a six-pack of beer in the icebox, and he's ready to watch the ball game. He's worked hard all week, and now he's ready to relax and enjoy himself. You think he wants to see a bunch of kooks with crazy signs?"

The very idea was absurd.

Whatever complaints the government may have about television, it should recognize that medium as one of the most stabilizing influences in the society, answering much of the needs of the leisure-time pressures brought on by shorter working hours. For a while "the problem of leisure" was a popular concern of social thinkers in the society, and fears were expressed about what the man accustomed to work would do when faced with the burden of free time on his hands. The problem is no longer much discussed, because it is obvious now what this man will do. He will get settled in front of the TV, put a six-pack of beer in the icebox, and turn on the ball game. For every hour of "live coverage" of the Vietnam War on television, there must surely be a thousand hours of the ball game.

For all practical purposes, the ball game is never over. In the spring and summer it is baseball, and winter and fall it is football, beginning shortly after lunch on Saturday and going into a second game that runs to dinner or after, and then the roundup of the games and the recaps and replays on the news, and then the whole thing again on Sunday, a vast swirl of bats, swings, passes, kicks, touchdowns, stolen bases, shown again on instant replay, slow-motion, split-screen, and isolated camera. There is no need to think, speak, or move. The ball game is on.

---

ii. *Playing ball is equated with Americanism; a team member is told to "do your demonstrating on the field"; a pep talk and prayer before the game*

Athletics are so intertwined with the nation's traditions that the American Legion sponsors baseball teams for boys as part of its program in "Americanism." Recently the more violent and action-packed game of football has seemed to replace baseball as the "national pastime," but both games are deeply rooted in the character of the society. They often serve as the introduction of boys to manhood, teaching physical stamina and courage, discipline, and team play.

Boys begin playing in vacant lots and backyards and playgrounds roughly as soon as they are able to walk and talk, but the first "big-time" training and experience in athletics comes in high school. All over the country, far outnumbering whatever new revolts or defections may be occurring, there are still young men coming up as they always did, learning to play the game, learning more than just blocking and tackling. A young man who played on a high school football team told me that he had several buddies who had planned to participate in a civil rights demonstration in their conservative midwestern city, but the coach talked to the boys involved and told them they had better not get mixed up in such a thing. "You do your demonstrating on the field," he told them.

The serious and almost sacred nature of the game can be felt in the locker room, especially in the hushed tension before the game begins. In the locker room of Shortridge High

School in Indianapolis, the Blue Devil football team was
dressing for its second game of the season, to be played under
the lights across town against Northwest, a new city high
school, and the team would be driven by bus to the game
after getting into uniform. They helped one another pull the
blue and white jerseys down over the massive shoulder pads,
and a few student managers helped some of the guys who
had to be taped. As each one got dressed he silently took a
seat on one of the two straight lines of benches facing one
another. There was the sound of cleats on the cement floor
and the rattle and bang of lockers being shut, a few calls of
"Hey, gimme a hand," all these diminishing, and then silence except for scattered coughs. Coach Benbow stepped to
the front of the room to say a few words. The coach, a former
lineman in high school at Muncie, Indiana, and then at
Butler University in Indianapolis, was a big heavy man
wearing a sport shirt and slacks and football cleats and holding a blue long-billed baseball cap to wear at the game.
Coach Benbow spoke quietly, without histrionics, and yet in
the hush of the room it was not without drama, in spite of
how familiar or maybe *because* it was so familiar, like a
ritual spoken through centuries, something from the ceremonies of manhood rites.

"You know this is an important game to us . . . this team
has a lot of experience . . . we're going to play each one as it
comes, and tonight we're only thinking of this one . . . remember you gotta hit and you gotta keep hitting . . . remember it's the second effort that counts . . . the second
effort, that's what makes champions."

Then he said the team would pray. The big Coach
crouched down on one knee on the cement, and there was a
clatter and shuffle as the boys scooted down from the benches
and knelt on the floor, some on one knee and some on both

knees, heads bowed, some holding their heads in both hands and pressing their hands against their temples as if for greater concentration, and after about thirty seconds of silence the Coach got up, and pulled his blue cap down on his head, and the boys got back up on the benches, although a few stayed on their knees longer than the others, and then they too got up, slowly, and the Coach said something to one of the managers about equipment, and then he turned to the team and said in a quick, loud voice, "We Gonna Beat 'Em?" and in unison, like the answer of a drill team, came a shouted, single-syllable "YES!"

And then the Coach, even louder, "We Gonna Beat 'Em?" and this time stronger and still louder, the unified team-pronounced "YES!" And then, lower pitched, businesslike, from the Coach: *"Let's go,"* and there is a general rise and push for the door, purposeful, serious, helmets tucked under arms, ready for battle, trotting out of the locker room and for the bus with that jog of assurance and importance appropriate for such occasions. I stood just a moment looking around the empty locker room, and noticed its one decoration, a painted board that must have been weathered and dusty from decades. It had a picture of a small dog and a large dog and contained that piece of locker room wisdom as hoary as if from some American version of Ecclesiastes: "It isn't the size of the dog in the fight, it's the size of the fight in the dog that counts."

Later I asked one of the young men who played on the team if they had always had a prayer before the game, and he said they had ever since he had been there, although it surprised him. I asked what he meant, and he said, "Well, I knew the reserve team prayed, because they get out on the field in a circle and have a prayer before the game. But the varsity doesn't do that, and so I figured when you made the varsity, you didn't have to pray. I was sort of surprised when I made the varsity and found they prayed too."

Not all the country has forsaken its faith. If the varsity prays, religion is not to be scoffed at.

And remember, the varsity won that night.

---

iii. *Businessmen serve the community and serve themselves lunch; Kiwanians hear about a suspicious new federal program*

The "meeting" is one of the principal forms of social and business gatherings in the society, and yet most of the meetings I have described thus far concern protest of some kind, and that is hardly typical. One of the representative types of meeting in the nation is that of the "service clubs," the organizations like Jaycees, Rotary, Kiwanis, and, at a generally little lower level of the social forest, the Lions, Moose, and Elks. These groups engage in good works, such as contributions and fund-raisings for charitable causes, awarding of scholarships, and civic improvement projects, but they are basically social in nature, and because membership is by selection, it is an honor bestowed, a badge of acceptance. So much do these groups enjoy meetings that most of them have a luncheon meeting once a week. On the outskirts of almost every American town or city you see right after the city-limits sign a number of colorful emblems of the service clubs stating the time and place and day of the week of their meetings, so that a traveling brother may join them if passing through and find good-fellowship among his own kind of people.

The service clubs are nonpolitical and noncontroversial, consisting of middle-class business and professional men who are the backbone of their community, the solid citizens who get things done. They sometimes like to hear controversial speakers at their meetings, in order to keep abreast of what's going on, but are unlikely to be moved to any sort of oddball sympathies. Donald Duncan, the former Green Beret turned antiwar crusader, said he often speaks at such gatherings, and finds that "they ask good questions, and usually afterward thank me and say that I've given them something to think about." When I asked what he advised people to do if they listened to one of his speeches and said they wanted to help end the war, Duncan smiled and said, "That's why I like to speak to groups like the Rotary. They don't ask."

During my stay in Phoenix, Arizona, I noticed that the local Kiwanis Club met every Tuesday at the Westward Ho, a downtown hotel, and I made some calls of inquiry and was graciously invited to come to the next meeting. In summer in Phoenix the temperature is usually over 100 degrees, and the businessmen dispense with coats and wear white short-sleeved shirts and ties (a resident complained to me that the ties were a recent innovation, an eastern influence that naturally was more uncomfortable than the formerly acceptable garb of open-necked sport shirts). So when I went to the meeting in the Turquoise Room of the Westward Ho, I was naturally identified as an outsider, since I was the only man in a suit. Nevertheless I was greeted pleasantly and given a seat at a table of ten men.

The conversation, as in many places that summer, concerned the urban rioting—a small disturbance had even struck Phoenix. Milton Sanders, an insurance man sitting on my left, was saying that, "the way things are going, if a kid threw a brick through a window, the federal government would probably give him a college scholarship."

Jim Patrick, president of the Valley National Bank in Phoenix, said he thought some of the businessmen ought to get together and start some project for helping get jobs for the people who needed them.

"Yes, but we'd have to have a screening committee," Sanders said, "so we'd know which ones were really qualified and which ones weren't. Some of those who don't work won't take menial jobs, but they don't have qualifications for anything else." He pointed to Mr. Patrick and said, "Some of them have a fifth-grade education and they want *your* job."

Patrick said nevertheless he'd like to get a hundred or so businessmen together and have each one hire two or three people from the slum area. He asked Sanders if he'd cooperate with such a plan, and Sanders said, "Yes, as long as you don't get the federal government into it."

Then the chairman of the program was introduced, a big square-jawed man described as a former All-America guard who played for the Packers and came to Arizona twenty years ago and has been in the cement business there ever since. "Bud," the former All-America, said he didn't know why he was chairman of the program today because the program consisted of some people from something called Upward Bound, and "I don't even know what that means, so I'll turn things over to Harry Matz, who is in charge of the Upward Bound group. Let's get him up here and find out what this is all about."

Harry Matz was a small, non-Kiwanian-looking guy with glasses who was wearing a suit. (I hadn't seen him when I came in.) He explained that Upward Bound was a project of the Office of Economic Opportunity, and gets 90 percent of its funds from the federal government and 10 percent from Arizona State University, where the program is conducted. There were 180 high school students in the program that summer, and "they are potential college students who we don't want to see drop out of school. We want both to sell them on going to college and prepare them so they'll be ready for it." The students were from families that might not have the money to send them to college unless there was scholarship help. The students in the program were 40 percent Mexican, 40 percent Negro, and 20 percent "uh-Anglo."

A young Mexican student in the program named Richard Estrada came to the microphone to tell more about it.

"The classes are more informal than high school," he said with obvious enthusiasm. "Students can say more what they believe. They teach us racial problems, religion, data processing, drama, all kinds of things. We can choose different courses, but all are required to take English and current events. We also learn about 'scientific thinking,' and we use a book called *Applied Logic,* and learn how to argue with the teacher, using logic and all."

Sanders leaned toward me and said, *"Sounds* like a federal program."

A few other students told about the program, and Mr. Matz said it had stirred great interest in the students, and that "we only have had two dropouts, and those were both because of work pressures from outside." He asked if there were any questions about the program.

The first question was how much did it cost.

Matz said it cost about $180,000 for the eight-week program for 180 students. There was a silence from the audience, and Matz said bravely, "Maybe that sounds like a lot, but if you measure it against burning Detroit, it's not much."

Sanders whispered to me, "If you just gave 'em the money it'd be enough to send 'em to college."

The questions were mostly of a skeptical nature, and Matz, almost apologetically, said, "I know it sounds kind of idealistic."

The All-America cement man came up and said to Mr. Matz, "We appreciate the time you've taken to come here, and we certainly took our time to listen to *you*."

There was perfunctory applause, and Sanders shook my hand as we stood up to go and said, "This was not a typical program today. Usually we have a good speech by a senator or congressman or someone like that. I guess we're in the summer slump."

❖ ❖ ❖

> The R. H. Macy Co. is trying out its first electronic salesgirl. This machine is smart enough to dispense 36 different items in 10 separate styles and sizes. It accepts one- and five-dollar bills in addition to coins and returns the correct change plus rejecting counterfeit currency.
>
> — *Howard Coughlin, President, Office Employees International Union, AFL-CIO, in* New Views on Automation, *86th Congress, Second Session, USGPO, 1960*

❖ ❖ ❖

Besides the presentation by the Upward Bound group, which some members found disappointing, the Kiwanis meeting had also included what the chairman called "the musical part of the program," which seemed to be generally well received. This featured a young couple who played piano duets of "Tonight," from *West Side Story,* and "Jamaica Rhumba," from I am not sure what. No matter how fine the execution, the piano duet is not among the more fashionable new art forms, nor were the selections played ones which have recently swept the nation's popularity polls. This preference for more traditional popular entertainment in music as well as in movies, books, and television, is firmly held by many middle-aged citizens who bravely resist the encroachment of the "new sound" and new sights of the pop-psychedelic vanguard.

It would be a mistake however to infer that any age or professional group or any area of the country is necessarily immune to the latest in entertainment and culture; the more swinging elements of the business and professional community in many towns and cities enjoy the most recent chic creations of the popular arts, and one doesn't have to be a hippie or live in New York or San Francisco to be in on what's in. In Phoenix, for instance, there existed not only the Kiwanis chapter, with its more traditional tastes in entertainment, but also a recently formed University Club, whose respectable business and professional members go in for more avant-garde entertainment at their gatherings.

I learned a little about the University Club from a bright young lawyer who belongs to the group and who took me for a drink at the lounge atop the new Del Webb Townhouse during my stay in Phoenix. The lawyer, Robert Bluemle, had just come from his Health Club after finishing up at the office, and was tan, well combed, freshly pressed, and completely unconquered by the withering late summer heat of Arizona. We drove to the Townhouse in his air-conditioned car, a standard appliance for Phoenix (one transplanted midwesterner told me that "down here, your wife doesn't ask you to turn on the heater in the car before a drive in winter, but to turn the air-conditioner on before a drive in summer").

Bluemle explained that the new University Club was formed "to serve as the hub of a group of people vitally concerned with the development of the city," but the interests of the members were not limited to local problems. For entertainment programs "we try to do things that are a little different," Bluemle said, and he noted that they had brought in speakers including John Ciardi, Emily Kimbrough, a composer of electronic music, and Fletcher Knebel. That seemed a fairly well-balanced mixture of taste, with Miss Kimbrough and Mr. Knebel representing the more traditional, while the electronic-music man and Mr. Ciardi had a more iconoclastic flavor. Bluemle said that Mr. Ciardi had talked frankly and informally about censorship and pornography, and in his authoritative and resonant voice Ciardi had discussed "fucking," using the actual word, which seemed to represent a breakthrough for guest speakers at Phoenix cultural events.

One of the most successful of the Club's cultural programs was a film series, and only recently Bluemle said they had a night of "underground movies," including such notorious avant-garde selections as *Scorpio Rising*, and a *Warhol Sampler*. He said the program had been received very well, and that he found some of the underground film work quite fascinating.

"Have you seen," he asked me, *"Window Water Running Baby Moving?"*

I confessed I had missed that particular film, and Bluemle filled in my cultural gap there by explaining it was about the birth of a child, and was "very impressive."

This appreciation of the avant-garde does not necessarily indicate a radical or unconventional taste in men like Bluemle or other sophisticated business and professional men in cities throughout the country, who enjoy keeping up with the latest pop cultural movements as they burst forth from New York and California. As far as important civic and governmental issues, Bluemle said, "One concern I think you'll find nationwide is a desperate attempt to find a solution to taxation, the problem of where the burden should fall.

There is increasing frustration for property owners—it seems like it's the middle-income businessman who now bears the heaviest burden in taxes." Another frustration Mr. Bluemle felt among his peers was about the war in Vietnam. "I don't think there's any deep conviction," he said, "that anything can be accomplished by it."

On the home front of Phoenix affairs, the University Club's interest in talks on pornography and censorship, and viewing underground movies, did not at all mean an abandonment of basically conventional social standards, and Bluemle mentioned that "we're fighting 'topless' now in Phoenix. We're trying not to become another Los Angeles." He said a number of housewives in the city had organized a Mother's March Against Topless, which was not an actual "march" of women wearing their "tops" on, but rather a petition campaign against the public display of "topless" entertainment.

Old and new, rear guard and avant, there seemed to be in Phoenix as in most American cities, wherever their location, a wide range of issues and entertainment, a heady array of civic and cultural concerns to occupy the time and energy of any interested citizen.

Topless Taxes Upward Bound, Window Water Running Baby Moving . . . March!

B. *Most men are moved by forces beyond themselves; you can't change the course of wars and hurricanes*

i. *A committee tries to speak for the "Silent Center," but a draft-board clerk does better*

The "Silent Center" is the term used to describe that vast middle ground of the populace, those people who go about their own business and do not wish to become engaged in controversy on one side or the other. They are often claimed by proponents of different sides of an issue, but by their very definition they do not themselves speak up for one side or the other. They do not form committees, but sometimes committees are formed in their behalf. This occurred after a great many antiwar committees were organized, including committees of professors, doctors, students, clergymen, and even businessmen, Feeling that the Silent Center had been neglected, a group of outstanding Americans formed a committee to speak *for* them. The new group, called "The Citizens Committee for Peace with Freedom in Vietnam," said in its announcement:

> We believe that the "silent center" should now be heard. Our objective . . . is not to suppress the voice of opposition. Our objective is to make sure that the majority voice of America is heard—loud and clear—so that Peking and Hanoi

will not mistake the voices of our dissenters for American discouragement and a weakening of will.

The committee said, again speaking not just for itself but for the tongue-tied citizens of the Silent Center, "We strongly support our commitment in Vietnam and the policy of noncompromising, although limited resistance to aggression."

Representing the Silent Center on the new committee were General Omar Bradley (ret.) and former Senator Paul Douglas (co-chairmen), former Presidents Eisenhower and Truman, AFL-CIO President George Meany, former Secretary of State Dean Acheson, well-known Negro writer Ralph Ellison, well-known white writer James T. Farrell, and many other well-known representative Americans from different fields. The committee's announcement did not say how it knew the feelings of the Silent Center, nor did it refer to a survey published the week before by the Gallup Poll which showed that 46 percent of the people questioned felt it was a "mistake" for America to have become involved in the war in Vietnam, an increase of 22 percent over the past two years. This of course did not mean that all those Americans *opposed* the war, for many who feel it was a mistake in the first place also feel that since the mistake has been made by their own government, the mistake has to be supported. However, even that sort of support would seem a lesser kind than the strong approval of the war policy expressed by the committee.

To see if I could learn a little more about the committee and its contacts with the Silent Center, the day after the announcement of its formation I called the telephone number of the Washington headquarters. The phone was answered by a pleasant female voice that said "Peace with Freedom." I asked to speak with one of the staff members, and the voice said with some surprise, "Oh, this is just an answering service."

She said there might be some people in the office later in the day, but I was already disillusioned. On the other hand, it seemed appropriate. If you try to reach the Silent Center, you ought to expect to get an answering service.

The committee was probably presumptuous in trying to give voice to the Silent Center, for by its very definition the support of that section of the populace lies in its silence, its quiet acceptance of what the authorities may ask it to do, its sense of the irrelevance and even inappropriateness of ordinary people presuming to support or oppose great issues of public policy. Voting is one thing, an anonymous and silent act itself, but once the people have voted, is it not up to those elected to determine great policies, and is it not the duty of the electorate to follow?

I felt that I gained a much better sense of the Silent Center from talking with a clerk for a draft board in Grand Rapids, Michigan. Miss Lucy Folkema, a petite lady with short blond hair and a neat blue suit, said she had worked for the Selective Service System for ten years and was now chief clerk of Local Board 42 of Grand Rapids.

I mentioned some of the antiwar demonstrations by University of Michigan students at the local draft board in Ann Arbor, and I wondered if any sort of protests had occurred here, or whether there was much resistance to the draft.

"It's different here than in Ann Arbor," Miss Folkema explained. "There have been the big demonstrations there, but you see, Ann Arbor has a different element of people. They have a large university there, and there are many different groups of people. In Grand Rapids, we're mostly a little Dutch community, and we have some Polish—of course, they're all Americans. Grand Rapids is a good community for raising a good, solid, concrete citizen.

"We have a lot of good institutions here in Grand Rapids," she said, "that help make it a good area to live in. There's Grace Bible College, and Calvin College, for instance. You get youngsters who have strong religious convictions. They're well aware that wars have been going on ever since Biblical times, and will keep going on."

There will be wars and rumors of wars, and this particular war of the moment in Vietnam is like most wars for the mass of people—part of the order of natural disaster, like flood or famine, illness or accident. They survive it as best they can, and would no more presume to alter it than to alter the course of a hurricane. These people are not without conscience, or dignity, or passion; what they lack is any notion that it is possible or even proper for ordinary humans to effect massive change in the course of great nations and their policies. They are not the movers of history but those who are moved, by forces above them—gods, or politicians.

✦　✦　✦

WITH JOHNSON IN THE FRONT PEW, MINISTER QUESTIONS WAR POLICY

The political complexities of our involvement in an undeclared war are so baffling . . . that I feel presumptuous even in asking questions.

But since there is a rather general consensus that something is wrong in Vietnam — a conviction voiced by leaders of nations traditionally our friends, leading military experts and the rank and file of American citizens — we wonder if some logical, straightforward explanation might be given without endangering whatever military or political advantages we now enjoy.

Relatively few of us plan even the

mildest form of disloyal action against
constituted authority. We know the
necessity of supporting our leader. . . .
While pledging our loyalty, we ask
humbly: Why?

— the Rev. Cotesworth Pinckney
Lewis, rector of Bruton Parish
Church, Williamsburg, Va., in a ser-
mon as reported by the New York
Times, November 13, 1967

✦ ✦ ✦

---

ii. *A hero who tried not to think about "why" so he wouldn't
go batty; another hero who never came home*

Robert L. Brown came hurrying down the stairs buttoning
up a starched white shirt, and invited me to take a seat on
the couch in the living room. He called to his mother in the
kitchen to ask when his little brother was bringing the car
back because he needed it to drive to work. Brown is a produce clerk in the Thrify Acres Market and also a minister in
the Church of the Apostolic Faith, Pentacostal, of Grand
Rapids, Michigan. He is one of ten children of a Negro
family, and he had recently returned from Vietnam, where
he served as a medical aide to a rifle company in the 25th
Infantry Division, and was awarded the Purple Heart after
being wounded by shrapnel and dragging five soldiers out of
the line of fire during an action near Pleiku. An account of
the battle in *Stars and Stripes* said that Brown "refused to
give himself morphine, even though he was in pain because
he didn't want to deprive someone else of it." He would not
be evacuated until all the other wounded were out of the
danger zone.

Brown told me he had refused to enlist in the Army because of his religious convictions, but was drafted and given
C.O. status.

"I said I would serve my country just as long as I could stay a C.O. and didn't have to kill anyone," he explained. "It seems like there's some law that I wasn't supposed to be in combat, but I think that's with the consent of the individual. They asked me if I wanted to go to Vietnam, and I said I wouldn't volunteer but if the Army wants me there I'll go."

I asked what he thought about the war after he got there, and he said, "The people there seemed pretty friendly, but you never knew who was who, as far as the enemy. I would say that me and most of the fellas more or less didn't know why we were there, but we had the idea we were asked to go there, and Congress passed this thing saying we would go. The fellas did their job because they were fighting for their lives."

He said he sometimes had his doubts. "One morning I woke up and thought, What am I here for? I had to put that outa my mind cause if I thought about it, it would have driven me batty."

Brown didn't know if others had such doubts, but anyway they didn't talk about it. "Mostly the guys talked about going home, reminiscing and all that. The Army kept us going with good supplies, and good food. We had steaks, fried chicken, veal, mashed potatoes with gravy, and they sent frozen ice cream into the field. We had a hot meal at least once a day, and a change of clothes every three to five days so we wouldn't get to feeling grubby. And our mail was always on time. We had packages from home, and that boosted morale too, so with all those things the fellas just couldn't be defeated."

I asked how he felt about it now that he was out and back home, and he said, "Well, when it all boils down, you wonder why we're there. I think it'll go on another nine or ten years. It's the kind of thing where we move 'em out of an area, and then they move back in again."

Brown said it was true that there were good race relations over there, and maybe that would have some effect back home: "I think it gave Southerners a better picture, I think some of them learned not to hate the Negro. I believe quite a few will never forget Negroes who fought next to them. Because of depending on each other that way, they could joke about things they never could if they were in the States."

He said he felt it was true that the service helped Negroes to achieve a better life when they got out: "Some branches train a man so he has a better chance for a job on the outside, and that's good. The thing that gets the Negroes down over there, and the whites, too, are the riots. It makes you feel, what's the use? I knew this one Negro man over there who said he was coming back and fight for the Negro cause in the States. He said we were first-class citizens when we were fighting a war, and we ought to be when we got back to our own cities, and he would fight for that whatever it took doing. He said if he could fight for a cause over there and kill, he could do it back home too."

The riots in Grand Rapids occurred after Brown got home from Vietnam, and he said, "It was going on about four or five blocks away. I'm trying to sleep and I hear shots, and even what sounds like machine guns—the same thing I heard in Vietnam, but it's even worse hearing it when you get back here. You figure you've got through it over there, and then you come home and hear it again."

Brown stayed home inside during the riot in his city. He said of his heroic action in Vietnam that "the Army brainwashes you—they say take a bunker, and the guys take it even knowing they'll get killed. I got it, too. When they yelled 'Medic' I moved. They stressed it was your job, the men were dependent on you, and when I felt I owed it to my men, it was a good feeling."

The article in *Stars and Stripes* said that instead of carrying a rifle, Brown went into battle carrying a walking stick and a Bible. He has no interest in taking part in the riots or revolts in the States for the cause of the Negro or civil rights or any of those things. His religion is more important to him than politics.

"My feeling is that *God* set me free, and so I have no limits," he said.

I thanked him for talking with me about these matters, and he called out again to ask where in the devil his brother was with that car. It was almost time for his shift to begin at the Thrifty Acres Market.

✦ ✦ ✦

What the outcome in Vietnam will be is anybody's guess, but whatever happens, Special Forces men will continue to fight Communism and make friends for America in the underdeveloped nations that are the targets of Communist expansion.
—*The Green Berets*, by Robin Moore

✦ ✦ ✦

CITATION
PURPLE HEART MEDAL
By direction of the President, the Purple Heart Medal is awarded posthumously to Private First Class Matthew D. Atkins III for wounds received in military operations in Vietnam, against hostile foreign forces, which resulted in his death. This award, first established by General George Washington in 1782, is presented as a tangible expression of our nation's gratitude and everlasting appreciation for Private First Class Atkins' gallantry and devotion in the service of his country. Private First Class Atkins stands in the unbroken line of patriots who have given their lives that our nation's goal of freedom and peace may be maintained.

—*Headquarters VI United States Army Corps*
The Federal Center, Battle Creek, Michigan

Private First Class Atkins had not wanted to go into the service; like so many other young men, he felt the two years would be wasted and he could accomplish so much more on the outside. He had just bought his own car, and was going to a local college and working at night. Because he had to work to put himself through college he could not be a full-time student and so could not get a student deferment and so was drafted.

Private First Class Atkins's parents live with their other three sons and one daughter in a small house in Grand Rapids where Mr. Atkins has a civil service job and Mrs. Atkins works at the Fisher Body plant of the General Motors Corporation and is a member of the union bargaining committee. Mr. Atkins was wearing a sweater and slacks and a pin of the United Auto Workers with a slogan for the current bargaining sessions that said, "UAW: United to Win Full Equality." The Atkinses are friendly but reserved people, people who had agreed to speak to a stranger about their son, of whom they are proud, and whose loss can never be remedied or relieved, and thinking this and seeing it I found myself more unable to speak than they were, and so they helped me.

Mrs. Atkins said that perhaps I wondered what her son was like, and she said, "As a child, he had such a big heart, he was always wanting to do something for someone else. He was the small one of the boys; our eighteen-year-old is five feet eleven and an all-round athlete. Matthew was the oldest, and he was not big or an athlete but he was always trying to stop kids fighting. He never talked back, and the teachers always complimented him on his citizenship.

"At first he really hated the Army," she said, "but I think he changed after being in the service a while. When he came home on furlough before going over, he said he didn't mind, and he felt attached to the other guys. I sometimes wondered if he was saying it just for our sake."

Mr. Atkins said that "he got his basic at Fort Knox and was transferred then to quartermaster school. He didn't have advanced infantry training, only basic, and I felt pretty bad when they put him in a line company in replacement over there after only one week of general training."

Mrs. Atkins said, "After he was there he wrote us that he wouldn't wish it on anybody. The temperature and heat were terrible, and he wasn't used to it. He told us how at Christmas he took candy and apples to the kids, and it was just like giving them a hundred-dollar bill. That made him happy. But he couldn't trust anyone—he said you couldn't tell if people who were friends during the day would be against you at night."

Mr. Atkins said that his own view of the war in general was that "if you ask me if we should be over there I say No. They talk about the Communist threat, but if they wanted to invade us they've got a stepping-stone in Cuba that's a lot closer. And if we're going to fight over there, as an ex-Army man myself, I say if you have the job get it done, don't place all these restrictions on how you can do it."

Mr. Atkins said that right after they heard of Matthew's death, "we were very bitter, we thought about moving to Canada. I felt like I only had one child when Matthew was taken, and I felt like 'You're not going to get another one.' But then I began to feel like the boys themselves should be able to choose, they should make the decision for themselves."

Mrs. Atkins said maybe I would like to see some of the letters that Matthew had written, and I said I would, and I copied down a few things from them. So these are a few fragments from the letters of Private First Class Matthew

Atkins III, of Grand Rapids, Michigan, who died of "wounds received in combat against hostile foreign forces" in South Vietnam:

> I just got back from a 10 day ambush patrol and for the first time got eight hours sleep. . . . I have been sleeping in swamps and on hard ground. . . .

> Don't worry about me Momma, God has taken good care of me. . . .

> Don't worry about me Momma, all the Viet Congs in the world couldn't keep me from coming home.

> Right now I'm in a foxhole on guard duty. The wind is blowing very hard and dust is flying everywhere. . . . This wind is too much and it's getting dark. Don't worry about me.

---

iii. *Some are silenced by the sheer weight of "fact"; a Californian suggests I forget the whole thing and find a yacht*

The people of supernation probably have more information available to them than the citizens of any country in history, and it is believed by many that the era of mass communications has created an "informed public" which has an opinion on everything, based on the vast agglomeration of facts poured out every day over television and radio, and in magazines, books, and newspapers. The common assumption is that citizens need no longer "take the word" of the government and indeed many do not, as indicated by the "credibility gap," a polite term roughly meaning the degree to which the people think the government is lying to them. At one point during my travels, a Gallup Poll found that 70 percent of the people surveyed did not believe that the government was telling the public all it should know about the war in Vietnam. (Interestingly enough, only 46 percent of the people surveyed on that occasion did not approve of the President's conduct of the war, which must mean that a quarter of the people thought the administration wasn't telling the whole truth, but supported it anyway, an indication of the depths of national loyalty.)

In addition to the "credibility gap," however, there is a less discussed phenomenon of communications which might be called "the informational glut," a by-product of mass communications which does not produce informed support or protest on any given issue but rather leads to the silence of confusion and resignation. The cross fire of charges and denials on a subject as controversial as the war, the contradictory "facts" reported by experts and on-the-spot observers, the daily onslaught of "news" about the war lead many educated people to throw up their hands and forget about it rather than attempt to sort out what they should believe and how they should feel from the hundreds of columns, books, news stories, television clips, radio broadcasts, Congressional debates, academic teach-ins, and military and political analyses published and broadcast and rehashed and criticized. In my travels I met a number of people, some of them college educated and intelligent, who had come to the conclusion that they simply couldn't possibly figure out what to believe about the war, that it was all too complicated to be sure enough about a particular position to take a stand, and so most of those people felt it best to leave things up to the government, whose job it was to figure out these matters and follow a course that was in the best interest of the people.

In a sense the government has contributed to this feeling by its different explanations of the very reasons why the war must be fought—or, as the administration says, its different emphasis on a variety of reasons at different times. Not only does the "emphasis" change on such matters as whether the nation is fighting to preserve the freedom of South Vietnam, or to contain Chinese aggression (or its potential aggression, in the case of Vietnam, since as yet China has no troops in that country), but even on more general interpretations of the war. The Secretary of State said in a speech to the American Legion last August that "our purpose in South Vietnam is very simple—there is no need for anyone to be confused about it—it is to prevent the seizure of South Vietnam by North Vietnam. Now that's not very complicated." This assurance that the purpose of the war was "simple" and "not very complicated," seemed a quite different interpretation than one contained in a Veterans Day message from the President to the gathering at Arlington Cemetery, a message in which he praised the men who fought in "this bitter and complex war." It does not even seem to be agreed on whether the war is "simple" or "complex," much less exactly why it must be fought.

The citizens' sense that the whole thing is beyond the understanding of the layman is sometimes further encouraged by the government's use of "technical" language about the war. When the U.S. forces first began bombing Hanoi, the government initially denied such action, but under intensive questioning by newsmen a State Department spokesman finally acknowledged that "in man-in-the-street parlance some targets could be considered to have been in Hanoi." This semantic defense of policy perhaps reached its zenith during one point of the questioning concerning the same issue, when a government spokesman asked in reply to a reporter's questions about the bombing of the city: "What is a city?"

The notion is presented that these are technical military

matters that "the man in the street" cannot understand, and which in fact are decided in what must evidently be a whole other language or "parlance" different from the common one spoken and understood by ordinary citizens.

What then is the "man in the street" to believe? He is often confused not only by government discussions of the war but also by critics of the war attempting to explain its background and history as a means of proving the unjust nature of the U.S. participation in it. The many academic "teach-ins" in opposition to the war seem mostly to have served as a kind of rally for those who already had decided the war was wrong, rather than as a means of influencing opinions of the undecided and the uninformed. One point on which both supporters and critics of the war can generally agree—with the evident exception of Dean Rusk—is the tremendous complexity of it. Not only the "man in the street" but many educated citizens have difficulty in understanding the tangled roots of the conflict, even when concisely explained. Perhaps typical of this difficulty is the report of a college student of average grades and intelligence who was assigned by a teacher to write up an account of a "teach-in" held in Boston. One of the speakers was a Harvard professor who outlined the history leading up to the present state of the conflict, presenting it in reasoned, orderly fashion, and leaving the student with the following understanding as conveyed in her account of the lecture:

> Beginning with the French National Convention in 1921, I began to realize that it would be virtually impossible for me to reconstruct the history of South East Asia but I made an attempt, as you shall see by reading further. As I recall it, Ho Chi Mein was the Indo Chinese deligate to the French National Convention, which seemed to be the touchstone leading to the current war. Ho Chi Mein's goal was to save

his country from what he called the "yoke of Colonialism."
Ho Chi Mein also became the founding member of the
Communist party in France, and in the twenties, the Communist party was very strong in Vietnam. These few facts
brought me up to the year 1939 when (and I quote because
I have no knowledge of what I am saying) "elections fell for
the Colonials in the southern two thirds of South Vietnam."
Eighty percent of the ballots were for Trotskiets. Then the
additional fact was thrown in that Trotskiesm was never supported by any government at any time. This would lead me
to the conclusion that the voting was in some way fixed,
although I'm probably incorrect. The next fact I gathered
with my speedy, yet not quick enough pen, was that the
Chinese occupied North Vietnam while South Vietnam was
British controlled. Then Ho Chi Mein set up the Republic
of Vietnam, although I don't see how this is possible since
it seemed that he only controlled the northern half. The next
important fact I gathered was that there was a powerful
premier called Diem who had lots of connections but no
popular support. Diem spent about twelve million dollars in
bribes, (to who I don't know), and became the new president,
(of what I'm not sure). Another election in the year 1955
occurred, the result being that eighty-three per cent of the
voters voted for peace as their goal, while four percent
wanted an immediate Communist victory. Also in 1955 Diem
launched a campaign of terror and "the countryside took
up arms in its own defense."

. . . . .

I enjoyed the speech very much, and although I am opposed
to the Professor's views, his speech certainly appealed to my
emotions very effectively.

That hodgepodge historical puzzle, with pieces missing
and others put in the wrong place, that Alice-in-Wonderland
interpretation which nevertheless "appealed very effectively" to the emotions of the transcriber, probably represents a better understanding (or misunderstanding) of the
historical background of the war than is held by the majority

of adult American citizens. The public opinion polls crank out the latest "news" of the sentiment of the nation, what the citizens feel about bombing the north or withdrawing the troops or allowing the National Liberation Front to participate in negotiations. But such polls are only glimpses through a looking glass, a mirror shaped by the understanding the citizen has been able to gain through the mass of often contradictory information conveyed by the mass media. A far more revealing and relevant type of poll might be conducted to discover not the citizen's opinion of a situation but his knowledge of it. In the case of the Vietnam War, the results might be especially illuminating and myth-shattering about the state of "informed public opinion" in a democracy during a time of the greatest means of communication in history.

Completely aside from the complexity and contradictions of communications about the war, the effect of what could be called "informational overkill" is as much a factor as any in discouraging people from trudging on in their quest for understanding, or from thinking about it at all. So much has been said that many have tired of hearing about it, and even the most conscientious have a hard time maintaining their interest and keeping up on the latest reports and controversies concerning the subject; interest rises, fades, perhaps rises again, but can hardly be maintained at a steady level of study and discussion and examination of the never-ceasing accumulation of facts and interpretations, especially when it is happening halfway around the world and its effects are so limited at home.

In Hollywood, a Sunday supplement writer loosened his belt after a big dinner and discussion of my assignment and, tired of the whole matter, yawned and scratched his belly and said, "Listen, the war doesn't have much effect at all. We sent a guy out to some little town in the Midwest to talk to people about it, but he didn't come up with much. If I were you, I'd go up to Santa Barbara for a few weeks and see if you can find someone who has a yacht."

In Detroit, a Ford Motor Company intellectual, employed on the "civic and governmental affairs" staff of the corporation, looked out the window of his office across the rolling green lawns of Dearborn and reflected: "What's going on in this country during the war? There's a tight race in the American League . . . Sky Divers are falling into Lake Erie."

In Bloomington, Indiana, a housewife and mother said honestly, "You know what really concerns me most at this moment? Whether to get my son a finished desk or an unfinished desk for his study." She said the whole subject of the war was too huge and complex to keep up with, and she felt the only thing to do was trust that the government was doing the best thing. She is intelligent and responsible—and in her own judgment there was too much she didn't know about the subject to make a decision.

The data are banked, the facts are filed, the statistics stored; more pile on each day, each minute, and the awesome mass of the information, the bulk and variety of which is overwhelming, becomes not only a means of informing the citizen but also a means of intimidating him. What can one man say confronted with all that evidence, evidence which never ends? Perhaps it is better not to judge, not to presume to give a verdict—other than the verdict of silence.

C. *Some elements of the population have been so subdued that they serve as "models" of successful pacification*

i. *"When you're over fifty, and you're feelin, sweet sixteen. . . ."*

There will be no riots in Sun City, Arizona. The 17,000 people who live there are what Miss Lucy Folkema might describe as "concrete citizens" from all over the country, mainly the Midwest, who have come to relax and reap the fruits of a life of toil and service to their families and communities by basking in the sun and the leisure-life activities of the nation's "first *active* retirement community."

"People say life is regimented here," said Jerry Svendsen, a blond young public relations man for the Del E. Webb Corporation, builders of Sun City, "but think how regimented *our* lives are, in everyday work. Sure there's a lot of activities, but they can do whatever they want. When a couple comes to Sun City, they throw away their alarm clock."

Mr. Svendsen, a sincere man much beset and troubled by adverse publicity from snide social critics of the planned retirement community, assured me that Sun City "gives people something meaningful to do. There's more than just bridge and golf."

I asked what else there was, and he said, "Lawn bowling, horseshoes, ceramics, whist, leathercraft, square dancing, pinochle. There's even a rockheads club. They go out and hunt for rocks."

To qualify for residence in Sun City at least one of the couple must be over fifty years old, and they must not have any school-age children living with them. They must also be able to afford one of the new specially designed homes, whose price range began at $9000 to $12,000, but with the demands for the type of home prospective citizens desired they now fall in the $12,000 to $25,000 range. The homes are specially designed with ingenious features attractive to the retirement set, such as electric outlets placed high enough in the walls so that it is not necessary to bend over to put in a plug, and "gravel lawns" for the man who has too long lived with the nagging necessity of mowing the grass.

We passed some homes with For Sale signs, and Svendsen said, "I'll admit Sun City isn't the answer for *all* retired people. There are forty million people over fifty years old in the country, and there are only three thousand retirement communities. Probably your major reason for moving is lonesomeness for children. Some people come out and get active, but others get maudlin. Others can't take the warm climate. Some move when they lose a partner."

We passed a rather obese lady riding a large tricycle. There are no children in Sun City.

After the tour, we went to a barbecue dinner that was being held in a restaurant in the shopping center for guests who had come to visit Sun City on the "Vacation Special" program, which allows a couple considering retirement to spend a week in the community for $75, in an apartment with kitchenette, and including breakfast and the barbecue dinner (not including travel). Svendsen said that 28 percent of the people who had come on the previous month's "Special" had purchased homes.

The restaurant was called The Melody Lane, and was a rather barren room whose walls were relieved on one side with some irregularly placed landscapes, and on the other side with emblems of the Lions, Kiwanis, and other service clubs. There were folding chairs and long tables, like the ones used at a church supper. There was no air conditioning, and outside it was 102 degrees. The guests, accompanied by resident greeters, lined up for the barbecue ladled out on paper plates.

After dinner Jerry served as MC, and first introduced the guests, who received a rousing hand of applause for the states they came from, which included Illinois, Texas, Oklahoma, and New Jersey. Someone pronounced the last state as "New Joisey," and everyone laughed.

Jerry introduced the Sun City Rhythm Ramblers, a band made up of the residents, and then Edna Lee and Harry Lee, who headed the Paws and Taws square dance club. They did a square dance. Then came Larry Armstrong, a "vocalist," and his wife, Marie.

Larry and Marie had come to Sun City as "singles" and are one of the community's love matches, who by their example hold such promise to other "singles" who might want to move there.

"Marie and I met in Sun City three years ago," Larry said, "and we've been singing ever since."

He said there was one song that everyone likes because "it sorta brings us closer to our families"—the children and grandchildren back home. Although the kids were gone, the song said, there was consolation that even though they were far away, they and their parents, in the evening, still have "the same silver moon."

Things like this recalled the fact that Sun City would have been impossible several generations ago, for then it was the custom for older people to live with their children in big "family" houses.

Larry then sang the "theme song" of Sun City, which he had written himself, a jaunty tune whose refrain was "When you're over fifty, and you're feelin' sweet sixteen. . . ."

Jerry had warned the audience that a reporter was present, and that most visiting writers had not given Sun City "the type of publicity" they would like. Then I had to stand up. After the program several people came up to me to ask me "what I was going to write." One lady said I was too young, it took an older person to write about it. A couple who belonged to the square dance group came up, and the woman asked that I not say anything bad about Sun City. Her husband said, "How could anyone say anything bad about it? There's everything here you could want."

---

ii. *"Being an Indian, I'm slow to think . . ."*

One of the most effective pacification programs in history was carried out in the late nineteenth century by the United States Cavalry. The native Indian tribes, descendants of peoples who had inhabited the land as long as 10,000 years ago, were hostile to the new white settlers who were taking over the continent, and these unruly "redmen" naturally had to be brought under control for the sake of progress. In the case of the troublesome Navajo tribes of the Southwest, a humane plan was developed in which the government sent the American cavalry hero Kit Carson to round up the Navajos and take them to Fort Sumner, New Mexico, where they would be taught a sedentary agricultural life patterned after the Pueblos, a tribe which had long lived in a state of cultural pacification. The Navajos were uncooperative and so, according to the U.S. Bureau of Indian Affairs, "to starve them into submission, soldiers killed their sheep and destroyed their cornfields and orchards." Even then, some fled and hid from the pacifiers, and finally the government negotiated a settlement with the Navajos, granting them a large "reservation" in 1868, where most have remained ever since. There are certain parallels with aspects of U.S. pacification in Vietnam, where entire villages sometimes have to be moved to another area, and mountain tribes have been transferred to different sites assigned them by the pacification forces. An important part of the pacification of the native American Indians included the sending of missionaries to teach them that their religious beliefs were primitive and their old customs were inferior and uncivilized. The white settlers also brought the Indians the gift of alcohol, and having been stripped of their land and heritage and herded onto reservations, the Indians took to the civilized intoxicant with a vengeance. This white man's contribution so affected the Indian culture that to this day liquor remains one of the major forces of disruption, illness, and death among the Indians. The white government and its missionaries, civil and religious, also succeeded in instilling a sense of deep inferiority that is still a predominant factor.

Of course the different tribes are in different stages of advancement today, and in Arizona I heard many white men praise the progress of the Apaches, who had developed a productive timber and tourist industry. One white businessman said in praise of the Apaches' adaptation to modern life, "They were the warriors, now they're the do-ers."

Even among different tribes, of course, "all Indians are different, just like white men," I was told by James Wallace, superintendent of the Phoenix Indian School. The school is a boarding school for children from reservations, and Wallace said it was one of the leading secondary schools in the country. As proof of its excellence he cited the fact that "we are the only high school band from Arizona to be invited to march in the Rose Bowl parade next year. This is an honor not many can achieve, as there are only thirty high school bands in the whole parade."

The Indians have served faithfully in the U.S. armed forces—I heard of no dissent among their youth about the current war—and Mr. Wallace boasted that "in World War II there was no better soldier than the Indian. They are very stealthy you know, they make wonderful scouts."

It is felt that service in the military is as beneficial to Indians as it is to Negroes, giving them training and opening up new horizons for them. Wallace said many ambitious Indians had been placed in factory jobs in recent years, and that they are particularly well suited to such work "because of their finger dexterity. Did you know the finger dexterity of the Indians is higher than that of any other race?"

Mr. Wallace gained his wide knowledge of Indian culture through a career of thirty-three years in Indian education, and is probably typical of the white men who have devoted themselves to this cause. I asked him how he had become interested in the Indians in the first place, and Wallace, a big, loquacious man wearing a white shirt and tie and a large Masonic ring, said he had graduated from Springfield College in Massachusetts and a relative who was a nurse in the Indian service in South Dakota helped him get a job with the Bureau of Indian Affairs at a reservation in that state. "It was 1934," Wallace explained, "and you were lucky in those days to be able to get a job as a ditch digger."

One evening I went back to the school to talk to Lee

Stevens, a young man from the Apache reservation at San Carlos, Arizona, who works at the school as a dorm supervisor and goes to the two-year Phoenix College at night and in summers. Stevens was a serious, intelligent young man, extremely courteous but extremely reluctant to talk very much. I asked about San Carlos and the Indian School, and after long silences a few things would be said, and then Stevens began speaking a little more freely, and told about his own vocational training, which seemed typical in the irony of its outcome. After high school he went to a vocational-training school sponsored by the federal government, and learned how to be a barber. He then, as is the plan in these things, returned to the reservation and opened a barbershop. The only trouble was the Indian men had always cut their own hair and saw no reason to pay money to have it cut in a barbershop. Eventually Stevens left and turned the shop over to another young man who had received his vocational training as a barber, and was not doing much better, the last Stevens had heard. Another young man, however, had been trained as a beautician and opened a beauty shop on the reservation which soon became fairly popular with the women. It seemed, however, that the training of Stevens and his successor in the barbershop was the sort of help too often given by well-meaning programs—training a man to perform a service that is not wanted by his own people.

I was very interested in all this, and was beginning to enjoy the conversation, when a young white man who taught at the school came in, and wishing to be helpful, bombarded me with all sorts of sociological theories, pamphlets, books, statistics, and academic jargon. Every once in a while he would turn to Stevens for confirmation of some point, and Stevens would always politely agree. I tried to get Stevens talking again, but he deferred to the white man, who had much more to say, and would answer any question I put. It was all on the order of his telling me that "there are ten sociological variables which influence why Indian students become dropouts."

He also showed me a paper he had written which concluded that the material he had read for the assignment "has been helpful in establishing a more equitable reference with Indian clients."

I said I had better be going, and Stevens walked out to the car with me. I thanked him for his time, and he said, almost spontaneously, though in a quiet, measured manner, "It's very discouraging trying to help the kids here, as a counselor. We try to get them to mix with other groups, to get involved in things outside their own society, and maybe they do just a little. Then they go home to the reservation in the summer, and in three months the parents undo everything you've done in nine months. Most of them only speak their Indian language at home, and they hear the traditional views of their parents, and they come back just as withdrawn as they were before."

He paused and then said, "The Indian problem is a very complicated, difficult thing," and it sounded as if he were talking about a deep and sensitive wound—and he was.

I visited the Salt River reservation outside Phoenix where the Pimas live, a tribe whose heritage is a peaceful one of irrigated farming and native artistry, with a special excellence in weaving and basket-making. I was taken around the reservation by Mrs. Anna B. Shaw, a silver-haired lady who is editor of *Awathm Awahan* (*Pima Letters*), a monthly mimeographed newsletter. Some of the tribal council members had been reluctant to talk to an outsider, but referred me to Mrs. Shaw, a Pima who has moved in the great world outside and knows how to deal with such matters. Mrs. Shaw, who puts out her paper from a small office in a converted trailer, told me she had lived in Phoenix for many years and taken part in the life of the community. She was invited to join the PTA, and she said, "At first I thought, being an Indian, would I be able to do it? Would I be able to participate and do my duties?"

She found she indeed was able to; Mrs. Shaw seemed in fact a quite remarkable woman, and in addition to putting out the newspaper, was writing up old stories and legends she had heard from her elders, so that they wouldn't be entirely lost, and also having old songs transcribed, some of which were no longer sung after the missionaries came and taught them Christian songs of worship instead. Someone at the University at Tempe was helping her publish the children's stories, and yet all this was told not only modestly but with self-deprecation, punctuated with remarks like "being an Indian, I'm slow to think."

Mrs. Shaw and I went to a lunch that was served every week on the reservation to raise money for a children's house the people had built, which Mrs. Shaw explained was mainly for children whose parents had too much trouble with alcohol. I was the only non-Piman at the lunch, and the others regarded me with a silent and withdrawn manner that seemed almost bordering on fear. The more sophisticated Mrs. Shaw tried to jolly them up, but not to much avail, and she apologized for their shyness afterward, but said they really didn't know how to act around strangers. She sighed, and said, "That's an Indian for you," a remark that always followed some story or instance of Indian "inferiority."

Yes, these people have been pacified well. I later heard about some young militant Indian men who carried cards that said "Red Power" and distributed bumper stickers that said "Custer Died for Your Sins." Maybe a new spirit of identity and pride will arise in the younger groups—perhaps helped by the new "fashionableness" of the Indians caused by the hippie-cult imitations of them; but in the meantime, it is easy to see that Kit Carson and his associates had done a very thorough job.

---

iii. *"My father built a wall . . ."*

In my travels in California I did not come across any Mexican-American, although I vaguely knew there were several million of them in the state. Occasionally I asked a white person active in liberal or antiwar causes if any Mexicans were involved, and they invariably said, well, they *intended* to get them involved but in the meantime, would I like to meet some Negroes. In Phoenix, Arizona, I made a point of what I had come to think of as "looking for Mexicans," and indeed was able to find some. I referred to my California experience, and my sense that the Mexicans were more isolated than the Negroes in America, when I talked with Joe Villa of the Community Council in Phoenix, and he said he thought that was true, and attempted to explain some elements involved in it.

"The Mexican-American to an extent ghettoizes himself— he feels more comfortable among his own kind and with his own language. I'll go back to my father's mentality to try to explain. When I was ten years old, my father built a wall. We lived in the inner city of the little town of Clovis, New Mexico, and he was building this concrete wall around the house. I worked like a peon on the wall, helping my father reinforce it with barbed wire and bed rails, and finally I asked him what it was for. He said, 'Bullets won't go through that wall.' He came from Mexico in 1916, and he was in the war of 1910 and knew killing and the dangers of war, and that wall was security to him—a reaction to what he came from. There is still this mentality, this need for security in many ways."

Villa was the twelfth of fifteen children, earned a degree in Inter-American affairs at the University of New Mexico, and now lives in Phoenix with his wife and their seven children. He was one of the key men in the development of the local poverty program and now as a staff member of the Community Council is active in social work and the affairs of the Mexican-American community. When the "riot" in its lesser form of "disturbance" hit Phoenix, it occurred in the Negro ghetto but did not spread to the Mexican-Americans, though Villa said it was very tense. The Mayor had responded to the outbreak by saying he had thirty new jobs available for Negroes. After that, Villa began getting angry calls from Mexicans who wondered why the Mayor didn't have any jobs for *them*.

"They were really stirred up," Joe said. "They were telling me, 'By God, if we have to throw a rock through a window to get some attention, then by God let's do it.' It wouldn't take much to get Mexican youngsters involved in that sort of thing. We have a few militant people on the scene, and they were saying the Mayor's statement showed that they had to riot, too, if they wanted to get anything. I called some of the militant people, and I told everyone that those jobs of the Mayor's were open to Mexicans too, and we did manage to cool it."

I asked if any of the young militants of the Mexican-American community were involved in any of the antiwar protests, as were some of the young Negro activists, and Joe said, "No, we don't have anything like draft-card burners or that kind of protesters. I think some of it has to do with culture. To show any sign of being afraid of fighting or dying is to take away from one's *machismo*, one's manliness. Getting out on a firing line is proof of one's *machismo*, and it would take a big change for the Mexican to feel any differently from that. I have a nephew who has got three Purple Hearts in Vietnam and he is volunteering to go back. There is also a great sense of patriotism among Mexicans, it is almost like religion. When Chavez had marches in the grape strike in Delano, California, you'll see he had people carrying flags and the cross—the patriotism and religion is tied up together and is very important."

Joe Villa is one of those rare men of any race or culture who has the ability of putting a stranger at ease, of talking in an open, relaxed manner that makes the stranger feel he is talking things over with a friend he has known for years, and so I was eager to accept his invitation to show me around some of the Mexican-American areas in Phoenix. We were accompanied by Manuel Fimbres, a young Mexican-American who also works for the Community Council, and as Joe explained when he introduced me to Fimbres, "Manuel has a Ph.D. from Boston College, and he was the first 'official' Mexican social worker in the city." He winked at me and said, "You can understand that at first we put him on exhibit."

The three of us drove late one afternoon through South Phoenix, taking in some of the landmarks like Friendly House, which Joe called "a kind of Americanization Center," where Mexicans study the Constitution and take classes to study for citizenship examinations. We visited the new southside headquarters of LEAP (the local branch of the poverty program), which was housed in a converted Safeway market, and brought together under one roof all of the independent service agencies. "Everything from Planned Parenthood to Catholic Social Services," Joe said, pointing to the directory.

We also passed another sort of landmark, the El Rey Cafe, a formerly "exclusive" Mexican restaurant which had discriminated against Negro customers, until Mexican leaders and the local Human Relations Council succeeded in cracking the "code."

"In the Southwest the Mexicans are a larger minority than the Negroes," Joe said. "And there is a lot of suspicion and resentment of the Negroes among Mexicans. The Negroes are more articulate, they are the ones who follow through on civil rights, and there is a fear that they will get all the jobs and opportunities that open up. Mexicans have voiced this fear in complaining about Negroes getting more of a share of the poverty program money."

Joe suggested we go by the JFK Community Center, located in a Mexican ghetto within a larger Negro ghetto. The LEAP program already had a community center in the larger neighborhood, but it was in the Negro part and run by Negroes and the Mexicans wanted to have a center of their own. The JFK Center was a small, one-story house on Jones Street, an easily missed dirt road. There was no name or sign on the house, and inside on the pink-painted walls of the anteroom were three decorations: a picture of Christ, surrounded by worshippers; a picture of John F. Kennedy; a framed front page of a Spanish-language newspaper featuring a letter of condolence on behalf of Mexican and other Spanish-speaking Americans to Mrs. Jacqueline Kennedy following the assassination of the President.

A little old man with a wrinkled brown face and gray hair sat at a card table with a small blue vase of flowers and a library book called *The American Continents*. The old man called in the chairman of the Center, a tall young man with a moustache, and Joe introduced us all around and said I was a writer who was interested in learning about the Center. At the back of the anteroom was a kitchen, and to the side was the main room, just large enough for a long table where a dozen or so people sat participating in an English class. The chairman pulled the card table over to a corner near the kitchen and away from the room where the class was being held so we wouldn't disturb it, although we could hear the rhythmic chanting of answers as we spoke: "Good eve-ning." "How-are-you?"

I asked the chairman what the Center did besides hold the language classes, and he said eventually they wanted to have a credit union, a clothing bank, and also develop a recreation program for youth—not just for Mexicans, but "Negroes and gringos" would be welcome too. The stockier man, who sat with folded arms and had the air of a sergeant at arms for the group, pointed to my notebook, and asked Joe Villa what the purpose was of this "investigation."

Joe hastened to explain that it was not an "investigation" but that I wrote for a *revistas* and was simply gathering material for articles. This seemed to satisfy the man, and he more freely joined the others in talking. It was around seven o'clock but still light and still Arizona-hot, especially in the ovenlike little house, and Joe, Manuel and I, the only ones with coats and ties, took off our coats and loosened our ties. The three men from the Center, even the old man, said they worked on "ranches" in what Joe explained was seasonal farm work—picking oranges and lettuce and cotton, although they said most of the cotton picking was done by machines now. They said the usual pay was 85 cents an hour for picking and a dollar an hour for driving a tractor. Some men worked for similar wages in some of the "posh" restaurants in Phoenix, they said, because there were many Mexi-

cans who weren't citizens and would work for less than minimum pay. The sergeant-at-arms man asked that I not use
their names in discussing this, and not mention the names of
any restaurants; it would make *"problemas."*

Later, Joe pointed out that many of these people do the
same sort of farm work as migrants but they live in one place
all year round, and so are worse off than migrants since there
are only four or five months of the year when work is available, and since many aren't citizens they aren't eligible for
welfare payments.

The migrants are usually thought of as the most underprivileged, most downtrodden of the Mexican-Americans;
but there always seems to be a layer beneath what society
considers the lowest layer. Again, this layer is invisible to the
society at large.

Among the Mexican-Americans, in some spots, there are
stirrings. There is Cesar Chavez and the dramatic grape
strike in Delano (although there has yet emerged no Chavez
in the cities, where most Mexican-Americans live), and there
are nascent political organizations, and scattered young militants, but all this is new and as yet mostly formless. The
Mexican-Americans are still pacified, and so command the
approval of many middle-class whites of the Southwest who
are angry now at the Negroes. As one businessman in
Phoenix put it, "You didn't see any Mexicans in on the
rioting. They're different. And you ought to see their homes
—they may be small and poor, but they keep their yards as
neat as a pin."

III

The problems of patriotism are found to be great in time of limited war; many citizens are faithful but confused

III

"It is out of relations that we come to be. We all have relations of one sort or another—family relations, social relations, community relations, international relations."
—Nobody Said It's Easy: *A Practical Guide to Feelings and Relationships for Young People and Their Parents,* by Sally Liberman Smith

✦ ✦ ✦

When I called up the press division of the Department of Defense to say that I wished to visit some U.S. military bases, Assistant to the Secretary Richard Fryklund said that would be no problem at all. "We've got 'em all over the world," he said. "Just take your pick."

Befitting the role of a supernation, the United States has a million troops stationed in thirty countries around the globe, maintains mutual defense treaties with forty-two nations, and furnishes military or economic aid or both to nearly one hundred different countries. It is the greatest supplier of armaments in the world, with an annual sale of military equipment to underdeveloped countries that totaled $900 million in the last fiscal year. This figure alone indicates the growing strength of supernation over its super-rival, for the Soviet Union's annual arms sales to other countries runs only between $500 and $600 million.

In order to bear this super-responsibility, the United States devotes 60 percent of its federal budget (the money supplied by taxation of the populace), or $75 billion a year, to expenditures for "Defense," which is the term given to all military production and activity. For the coming year, its generals and admirals would like to have $98 billion. An outsider might well imagine that supernation exists in an extremely hostile world, surrounded everywhere by threatening enemies, for that would seem the simplest explanation for the necessity of such a vast deployment of arms and men in the cause of national defense.

This tremendous investment in the nation's defense, however, is not so much a drain on the economy as a stimulant to it, directly providing 10 percent of the entire employment of the population and aiding the continuance of what Ronald Steel, a former U.S. Foreign Service Officer, described as "an affluence that could support whole nations with its waste." It should be noted, however, that the really poor people seldom get even the "waste," and that in the midst of the national affluence acute malnutrition was found to be commonplace among the Negroes of rural Mississippi by a team of visiting doctors, and similar conditions exist throughout the rural South and Appalachia.

Ironically enough, some of the waste or spillover of that affluence which springs in significant part from the military-primed economy helps support some of the society's most dissident, antimilitary elements, such as the hippies. A concrete example of the "waste" of affluence supporting a protest element within the society is provided by a group of antiwar demonstrators who have kept up a "peace vigil" at the naval ammunitions installation at Port Chicago, a harbor north of San Francisco which serves as the principal loading point for shipment of bombs, napalm, bullets, and other ammunition to Vietnam. The "vigilers" who picket at Port Chicago live in an informal, cooperative sort of setup in a house in Canyon, California, and they are able to survive on a small budget of contributions from antiwar sympathizers because most of their food is free. They mainly eat what they call "Behind-the-Safeways" food, which is produce rejected because of partial spoilage such as a brown spot on a head of lettuce, an overripe tomato, or a partially spoiled banana. This food is put out in boxes behind the Safeway Super- market in San Francisco to be collected and thrown away, but the vigilers pick it up, the women cut out the bad parts and use the rest for meals that provide the main sustenance of the group. As one of the vigilers explained, "This country is so rich, you can live off the scraps from the table."

The effect on the general national affluence if the single biggest item of government spending (defense) was elimi- nated would obviously be catastrophic, and few responsible men consider such a perilous situation possible. And yet, with their awesome responsibilities, the leaders of superna- tion must consider every possible crisis, and so, just as one of their theorists has engaged in "thinking about the un- thinkable" prospect of total war in a nuclear age, so one of the leading industrialists has considered the perhaps even more unthinkable prospect of total peace. A. Carl Kotchian, President of the Lockheed Aircraft Corporation, one of the largest contractors of defense spending, explained in a paper on the subject that the possibility of total peace was "so unlikely that we might be tempted to dismiss it as a dream. And yet among the new breed of systems analysts and fore- casters in the aerospace industry, no possibility is too un- likely to be considered."

Considering the effects of a hypothesized "collapse" of de- fense production on Southern California alone, Mr. Kotch- ian said it would be "an economic setback of the first order. Fortunately, it will not bring collapse. Given the conditions of gradual disarmament extending over a period of fifty years or more, there will be no earthshaking strains on the South- ern California economy."

While it had to be admitted that total peace was eventually possible, "perhaps in one hundred years, perhaps even in fifty," Mr. Kotchian could confidently add, "but certainly not tomorrow or the day after tomorrow."

Even an end to the Vietnam War would of course not mean an end to the basic defense production of the nation. Everett Hayes, a public relations official of Lockheed, pointed out to me that supplies produced for that war might decrease in volume if the war ended, but such equipment would still be produced because it was not being made for that war alone; the production of helicopters, for instance, would continue and be further developed because "those are not just for use in Vietnam; they are part of what is necessary for the time we live in—the time of limited war."

This condition of nonpeace, a state of perpetual war preparedness, is the premise on which the conduct of nations is now based, the framework which men regarded as "reasonable" seek to operate within rather than to modify. Some men accept this situation not only because they feel it is the only possible arrangement for the survival of the most powerful nation in the world, but also because they feel it is the one which is on balance the most beneficial to the society as a whole. The recently published *Report from Iron Mountain on the Possibility and Desirability of Peace,* purportedly drawn up by a "Special Study Group" secretly appointed by the federal government, reached the conclusion that peace was in fact neither feasible nor desirable. Of course the Report was only a spoof; and yet its logic and conclusions were so "realistic" that it was taken at face value by many readers, including reviewers for some serious journals, as well as some government officials. A State Department official who read the book confessed to an interviewer that "I got further than I like to admit before I was certain that there was nothing at all factual behind it."

Fact and fiction are difficult to delineate, and it is difficult for citizens to know what to think about the era of wars that seem limited in justification as well as in strategy. In the two great world wars they fought before becoming a supernation, the people were sustained by the knowledge that the war was being fought to end all wars, and that made it worth doing, for their children, and their grandchildren, and for the peace and safety of the world. But now they have to learn that the war they are fighting is part of the complex burden of being a supernation, and that it might not bring an end to war at all. That is a hard thing to learn, but some leaders feel the people have learned it. General Omar Bradley (ret.) returned from a fact-finding mission to Vietnam, and he was much encouraged, not only about the way the war was going, but also about the ability of the people to understand and accept such wars. The general wrote: "We are a free people, a learning people. As Pilgrims we learned to farm. As colonists, we learned the wilderness. As victors, we learned that the end of a great war does not mean peace."

It means, instead, the new kind of war that is limited in aims as well as in area, one that does not necessarily seek an "all-out" victory or ask for all-out support and sacrifice from the citizens. This sort of war is frustrating not only for the "dissenters" but also for the "patriots," and having considered the problems and attitudes of the former group, we should now give attention to those of the latter.

It must be emphasized that the term "patriotism" is being used here in its most commonly accepted sense, which is more narrow than the dictionary definition of the word as "devotion to country." It is perhaps unfair but nonetheless true that citizens who oppose their country's policy in time of war are classed according to the basis of their opposition. That is, if a loyal citizen is opposed to the policy on the grounds that the country should *withdraw* from the war, he is thought of as a "dissenter." If another loyal citizen opposes policy on the grounds that the country should *increase* the war effort, he is considered a "patriot," along with those citizens who support the policy of the government as it is being carried out. If the "patriotic" type of critic becomes extreme in his demands that the war be extended and escalated, even to the point of charging that the government's own leaders are holding back because they are disloyal or duped by subversive elements, he still does not become a "dissenter," nor does he lose his status as a "patriot." Rather, he is reclassified in popular terminology as a "superpatriot."

Using this common conception of the term, we shall now look at some of the dilemmas of patriotism in a time of limited war.

A. *The home fires of patriotism, with limited fueling from the government, burn in varying degrees of intensity*

---

i. *A call to arms is issued for fighting the enemy at home as well as abroad; survival measures include storing up on "beans" (lots of them)*

"FELLOW-AMERICANS! We are at WAR! This war has been forced upon us by the declaration and designs of Anti-God Communism. In war there is only one alternative to Defeat—and that is VICTORY! So let's get on with it then—VICTORY—not only in Vietnam—but VICTORY OVER ANTI-GOD COMMUNISM the world over and MAY GOD BE WITH US!"

—*BREAKTHROUGH*, P.O. Box 3061, Detroit, Michigan

J. Donald Lobsinger is a quiet, intense young man who lives with his parents and works as an accountant in the finance section of the Department of Parks and Recreation of the city of Detroit, Michigan. In his off hours, Lobsinger is the founder and leader of a militant anti-Communist movement called Breakthrough, which most dramatically carried its message to the public in a protest against the performance of the Moscow Symphony Orchestra at the Detroit Art Institute in October of 1966. On that occasion, Breakthrough members passed out leaflets saying "Soviets! Go Home! Russian Communist Orchestra Not Welcome Here! Not While Our American Boys Are Being Killed by Russian-Armed and Russian-Supplied Communist Forces in Vietnam." But it was not the picketing or distribution of leaflets that focused public attention on the protest. The real drama occurred when Lobsinger and three of his followers leaped to the stage at the Art Institute auditorium during the concert, waving banners and shouting to the audience, as Lobsinger recalled the message, "Why applaud murderers of our boys, murderers of Christians?" This guerrilla action at least temporarily halted the performance until the Breakthrough demonstrators were led offstage by police and the musicians were persuaded that they could continue without further interference.

Lobsinger and his group had continued their campaign against Communism at home and abroad, and after the Detroit riots they had organized rallies to alert citizens to the Communist guidance of the uprisings and instruct the populace on how to prepare for the next outbreaks, which Breakthrough warned would be a Communist bid for a complete take-over of the nation. Lobsinger hired a hall with a 300-person capacity for the first of these public sessions, and he said that more than 800 others came who had to be turned away. This response proved, Lobsinger said, that the people of the city "are not buying the story of the riot as it's being told in the press and by government officials," and that "the people are frightened, and they have a right to be."

After the first public meeting, and before a series of others were scheduled to meet the demand for similar riot-defense instructions, Lobsinger was invited to address a luncheon meeting of the Friendship chapter of the Detroit Lions Club, and I received permission to attend this gathering. The Friendship chapter meets each Tuesday at 12:15 P.M. at the

Golden Galleon, a restaurant-bar which provides the Lions with a private room off the main dining area for their weekly functions. I arrived before Mr. Lobsinger, and explained to one of the Lions that I had come to hear the speech. The Lion said, "Do you have a gun?" and I assured him I did not, and the Lion explained that a lot of people didn't like Mr. Lobsinger.

Cleared of intent to assassinate, I was allowed to take a seat at a long table seating eighteen men, was bought a drink by a hospitable Lion on my right, and observed the few Lion ceremonials that followed the luncheon special of beef stew or veal cutlet. The chairman finally introduced Mr. Lobsinger, and said that Breakthrough was "an organization I am familiar with, and very much in favor of." He said the speaker would discuss the "recent civil disorders in Detroit."

Mr. Lobsinger, a thin, dark-haired man who spoke calmly, with great sincerity and a sense of intense urgency, said the half hour allotted him was hardly enough to explore the subject but he would do his best.

"What happened in Detroit this summer was not a 'riot,' " he said. "It was merely a training exercise by Communist-trained and Communist-equipped guerrillas, as part of a violent revolution. . . . When the *real* riot comes, it will be far worse than what happened this summer."

He said that citizens must take their own steps to prepare for the coming uprising, because "the last one showed that citizens can't safely depend on government officials for their protection and defense. If American people want to preserve their freedom, they have to face this."

There were two main things that citizens could do to get ready for the next outbreak: (1) "arm" and (2) "prepare for survival." Lobsinger said, "You have just seen the preliminaries, and the next one will be a revolution. Utilities will be cut off, the lights, the water system." He passed out a mimeo-graphed sheet which contained "Suggestions for Survival During a Period of Prolonged Civil Disorder." It said that each family should have, as a minimum for survival, a month's supply of food and essential items on hand. Among the suggested supplies listed were:

> Beans (lots of them) . . . Lots of canned foods . . . Brewer's Yeast (one bottle) . . . Pet food (if needed for pets) . . . canned milk (evaporated) . . . Whiskey (medicinal purposes) . . . Coleman stove (operates with kerosene) . . . Toilet paper . . . Soaps . . . First Aid Books . . . Hair-cutting tools. . . .

The instructions asked citizens to "organize your own block and make sure that every family has a ONE MONTH supply of food. . . . Should a neighbor be discordant or uncooperative, let him be. BEWARE OF THOSE WHO OPPOSE SUCH PREPARATION."

Again stressing that the citizens could not depend on their government to defend them, Lobsinger said, "In the riot last summer the Mayor said on the radio that 'life is more impor-tant than property.' That meant that the life of a looter was more important than the property of a law-abiding citizen.

"The reason the thing went so far was that government officials were either too cowardly to enforce the law, *or* this was part of a conspiracy to make it necessary to bring in federal troops, so people will get *conditioned* to look for federal troops, and feel they need them." He said this was part of a trend toward "federal control of our individual lives."

In the question period following the talk, someone asked if there wasn't a fella some time back who warned us against this Communist business, a man named Gerald L. K. Smith. Lobsinger said, yes, there was such a man, but he had tried to put all the blame on "just one race, and that wasn't right." Lobsinger said you shouldn't try to blame the Jews, as Smith often did, nor even should you blame the Negroes, "as a race."

"Most Negroes are loyal Americans," he said. "Many soldiers killed in Vietnam are Negroes, and many here oppose the black terrorists, but those loyal Negroes will be the first victims. They will be terrorized into submission."

Lobsinger said that when the real revolution came it would hit many cities through the nation all at once, and even if the government wanted to defend the citizens, there wouldn't be enough troops. "The men and children will be slaughtered," he said, "and the women will be raped. The women will be the reward for the terrorists."

Someone asked what could be done about allowing the *right* people to purchase firearms. The questioner said the manager of a sporting goods store told him that one day nine Negroes came in and bought high-powered rifles. Lobsinger said this was indeed a dilemma, but "the terrorists will get weapons one way or other. We have to be opposed to laws requiring registration of firearms, because we have to let loyal, decent citizens have a chance to arm for their own protection."

After the meeting broke up I stood around waiting to talk with Lobsinger, and one Lion in a short-sleeved sport shirt nodded at me, and said, "We're way ahead of him." I asked what he meant, and the man said, "He says to 'arm.' Hell, on my block we're already armed."

When most of the Lions had left, Lobsinger sat down with me at a table where he had piled some of his leaflets, and said he'd be glad to answer any questions. I asked how he first became interested in the cause of anti-Communism, and he said he was stationed in Germany when he was in the service, and he went to the eastern zone of Berlin once on a leave and "saw the hopelessness on the faces of the people." He felt for a long time there must be something people could do to fight Communism, and three years ago he formed Breakthrough. He didn't necessarily believe that the U.S. government was infiltrated with traitors, but that on the record of the past twenty-five years it certainly seemed the nation's leaders lacked the will to fight Communism, maybe because our own system had become so socialized, and so much like the Russians.' He said Breakthrough was criticized for its demonstration at the Moscow Symphony performance, but he asked, "Could you imagine us having a Nazi orchestra perform here during World War II?" He said we were supposed to be in a war against Communism, and therefore shouldn't it be an all-out war? He showed me a leaflet called "Victory in Vietnam" his group had put out, which said that the United States must get on the offensive and that "to win—we must abandon the absurd notion that Soviet Russia is a potential ally"; and it urged the United States to support the return of Chiang Kai-shek to the mainland of China.

Lobsinger talked calmly, and with evident conviction. I knew that among respectable, responsible people in Detroit he was considered a "crackpot," and his disruption of the Moscow Symphony was still joked about by sophisticated citizens. It occurred to me, however, that in fact a performance by a cultural delegation from an enemy with whom the country was engaged in all-out war, such as Nazi Germany in World War II, would indeed never have been tolerated. Certainly Americans had been told by their government that Communism was a worldwide conspiracy, that Russia as its leader was the principal enemy of the United States, that Chiang should return to his rightful rule on the Chinese mainland. If emphasis of those positions had been shifted, or played down, or no longer mentioned, how was Mr. Lob-singer to know that he should no longer believe them? If indeed, as the government said, the United States was fight-ing in Vietnam to stop the spread of Communism, why should loyal citizens applaud and entertain the representa-tives of that enemy conspiracy? At the least, it might be said in behalf of Mr. Lobsinger's sanity and sincerity that being a patriot had become a very complicated business.

ii. *A molder of limited-war policy defends it with limited rhetoric; it is found that there are "hawk do-gooders"*

I was born on July 4, 1776. . . . The Declaration of Inde-pendence is my birth certificate. . . . I am a nation.

You can look at me and see Ben Franklin walking down the streets of Philadelphia with a loaf of bread under his arm... you can see Betsy Ross with her needle. . . .

I am Babe Ruth and the World Series. . . .

The words were spoken by a single strong voice, and in the background the United States Navy Band Sea Chanters hummed "My Country 'Tis of Thee." When the recitation was concluded, the guests in the large banquet room of the Sheraton Park Hotel in Washington joined in a standing ovation. The guests were members and their wives of the National Defense Executive Reserve, a group of more than 2,500 executives from private business and professional life who are recruited and trained by the federal government "to step into key federal war jobs in an emergency." As the NDER explains the reason for its need, "In today's world the United States enjoys no geographical protection. The full fury of nuclear war could strike without warning, or limited war could demand full mobilization of the Nation's resources." Executives with expertise in the appropriate field are chosen to be ready for emergency service in government departments ranging from Defense to Agriculture, for tasks which, in the case of the latter department, would include "assessing attack effects on agricultural resources; and estimating needs for and claiming manpower, materials, equipment, supplies, and services."

The executive reservists had come to Washington to be briefed in operations of the departments to which they would be assigned in an emergency, and were concluding their two-day conference with the evening banquet, which featured entertainment by the Sea Chanters, the U.S. Marine Band, and a speech by General Maxwell Taylor (ret.), one of the architects of the nation's Vietnam policy. The mood of the evening was highly patriotic, not only because of the nature of the organization and its responsibilities of service to the nation, but also because of the reaction to the antiwar March on the Pentagon which had taken place just two days before the conference. The Navy Sea Chanters made indirect reference to that event after they sang:

> America you command and we'll obey
> Whatever it may be . . .

and one of their number stepped to the microphone and said, "These words make good sense these days. We believe in them, and we feel that the Americans who do believe in them outnumber by ten to one or twenty to one those *others* who get most of the coverage in the press." Those "others" and their latest demonstration were also a topic of conversation at the table where I sat. The wife of one NDER staffer summed up the feelings of many present concerning that subject when she said, "I don't see why we have to pay so much attention to a bunch of snotty-nosed kids."

The traditional all-out patriotism of the entertainment and conversation, however, was somewhat in contrast to the main address by General Taylor, which was not the old-fashioned type of inspirational glory-and-flag rhetoric, but exemplified the new style of "limited war" oratory. Calm and reasoned, unemotional and legalistic in presentation, the essence of the appeal for support of the war policy was not so much that it was a great and noble cause, but rather that it was, under the circumstances, just about the only thing the nation could do. The title of the speech, representative of its tone, was "Alternatives in Vietnam," and the conclusion was that there weren't any.

General Taylor said that there was disagreement about what we were doing in Vietnam, but that "our policy is clear. . . . We have an objective and a strategy. The strategy is designed to attain the objective."

This was the sort of cool, logical thinking that reasonable men would find difficult to quarrel with, and set the tone of an appeal to reason rather than emotion. The General went on to state the "objective" as being "the independence of South Vietnam and its freedom from attack. We only want the people allowed to guide their own country in their own way. We stand for the cessation of Communist aggression from the North and the right of self-determination. . . . That is our overall objective."

The General did not make any mention of the containment of China for the security of the United States as part of the objective, and a reporter at my table whispered, "He's out of date—he evidently didn't hear Rusk last week, or he's using an old speech." Secretary of State Rusk had recently made his much publicized statement that the U.S. military action in Vietnam was necessary to halt the aggression of China, which represented a threat to U.S. and world security, citing the specter of "a billion Chinese armed with nuclear weapons" in the near future. The Rusk statement was criticized for raising "the old yellow peril," or fear of Orientals on a racial basis, a charge which was vigorously denied, and in the following weeks administration officials turned the criticism around by suggesting that *withdrawal* from Southeast Asia would be a "racist" policy. As the Vice President put it, if the nation forsook its presence in Asia and concentrated its defenses in the West, it would mean that the United States really only cared about people whose "names and skin color are more like our own." Some critics of the Rusk statement charged that the government had changed its rationale for the war from the aim of defending South Vietnam against aggression, to the aim of containing Chinese aggression in the interest of U.S. security, a charge the administration denied by saying that *both* those aims were the reason for the nation's participation in the war, and always had been, but the first reason had simply been emphasized more often.

General Taylor at any rate did not mention anything about containing China, but presented in orderly fashion the different alternatives to the present U.S. policy that had been suggested, considered the effects of each one, and then gave reasons why he felt they would not be effective. Most of the arguments defending the policy had been made many times, but the general did seem to have a new argument against U.S. withdrawal. He said that this would have a very bad effect on the United States at home, for when France withdrew its troops from Vietnam, "the outcome" on France itself was "Gaullist authoritarianism." Though the general didn't say so, the implication seemed to be that De Gaulle had seized power in some military coup and was running France without constitutional government, an implication that was strengthened when the general said that if the United States, like France, withdrew from Vietnam, "we would have serious changes in our whole method of government"—evidently as France had supposedly had under "Gaullist authoritarianism."

General Taylor went through the range of alternatives from withdrawal to escalation, eliminating all as unsound, and concluded that any of the proposed changes would be "more serious than staying on our present course." The audience rose to applaud this reasoning. The speech was limited to Administration logic, and lacked any sign of passion, but there seemed to be an emotional carry-over from the performance of the Navy Sea Chanters and the U.S. Marine Band. The evening may have provided a workable formula for future limited-war celebrations: talk softly, but carry a big brass band.

✦ ✦ ✦

WAR MOTHERS PLAN
CONVENTION IN CITY

American War Mothers who were organized in Indianapolis in 1917 will celebrate their 50th anniversary beginning Sunday at the Sheraton-Lincoln. . . .

A memorial service will be conducted Monday, and Tuesday will be awards night for hospital volunteers and membership. "American War Mothers a Go-Go," on Wednesday evening, will be followed by a formal banquet and installation of officers on Thursday.

— *the Indianapolis* News

✦ ✦ ✦

Asking support for a war policy on the ground that, as General Taylor stated, alternatives to it would be "more serious," in the sense of worse for the country, is not the most glamorous sort of appeal to patriotism, and yet many citizens respond to it, out of a sense of duty and loyalty if not out of passion or deep conviction.

The government begins with an automatic base of support, an instinctive assumption on the part of most citizens that their own country's behavior must be right in relation to any country it opposes. Beyond a belief in the national "rightness," many people hold to the concept of loyalty expressed in the phrase "My country right or wrong, my country." This is a fairly common sentiment, expressed in family terms by the old saying "Blood is thicker than water," or, in G. K. Chesterton's parody of unquestioning national allegiance, "My father drunk or sober, my father."

This sort of responsive loyalty is one of a number of important "built-in" elements of support that the government can count on. One of these significant built-in factors is the death of the nation's own men, and in this war, as in others, that is a self-perpetuating element. Mathematicians could probably work out an equation for this principle, showing that the more men who are killed in a war, the more difficult it is for the government to call a halt to the war without an "honorable"—that is, victorious—solution. The deaths incurred in the war become in a sense a justification of the war's continuance. This common and quite human reaction was explained by a sophomore college student who wrote in an essay for her English class that "I have a cousin and a few friends over in Vietnam fighting now. One of my friends met his death there. . . . As I see it, if it was important enough for him to die for, then who am I to protest? On the contrary, there is now good reason to fight. Namely, to give his death a significance."

"That these honored dead shall not have died in vain . . ."

Another kind of patriotic support in the era of limited war might be called the "progressional involvement" concept. In a sense this concept matches the government's step-by-step measures of escalation that promise to bring the conflict to a satisfactory conclusion, and then when the measures fail, the escalation seems impossible to abandon without disaster and becomes its own justification. Many newspaper editorial pages have followed this route, and the feeling about it in one case was explained by Jack Spalding, editor of the Atlanta *Journal,* in discussing what he termed the rather "hawkish" stand of his paper. "We were for escalation," he said, "for escalation as a means of bringing 'em to the bargaining table. But it sure as hell didn't. We were optimistic then, but now I'm not. I don't see any end to it. Debate about our being there is over, at least among the people I talk to. We've gone too far to change things. There's no sense looking back, no sense debating the philosophical aspects of it. That should have been done ten years ago."

Remarking on the new and unfamiliar atmosphere attendant on a limited war, Mr. Spalding observed that "in the last few months two friends of mine have lost sons in Vietnam, and I have two nephews in uniform. It gets to you that way, but except for that it still doesn't feel like we're in a 'real' war."

Ray Tardy, a Negro veteran of the European and African theaters in World War II, who has conceived and executed some particularly effective and imaginative social and educational programs as director of the poverty program in Grand Rapids, Michigan, said that "there's been no all-out movement for patriotism in this war. Myself, I keep a box of American flags in the house, and I give 'em to the kids to play with, so the flag and its meaning gets imprinted on them. On flag days, we don't see enough flags out. We've been giving them away free for people who will fly them— we'll come over and put one up for anyone who wants one."

When I talked with Tardy one late summer Sunday after-

noon in his living room, a Detroit Tigers game was on television, and he illustrated his own feelings by saying, "We've
got a team in Washington, and we have to back 'em the same
way as I have to scream for Sparma [the Tiger pitcher in the
game] and the Tigers. Right now, the Tigers are losing, and
I don't like it. That's a Michigan team, that's *my* team. Same
way with the team in Washington [the federal government,
not the American League Senators]. When anyone talks to
me about the war, I tell 'em real quick—Johnson is your
man, our man. If an election changes it, that's a different
story. If someone else is elected, then *he's* our man."

Many supporters of the war do not have the "team" spirit
that Tardy does, but share his feeling that it is necessary to
fight "over there" in order not to have to fight on his nation's
own ground. "One thing I learned personally in World War
II," Tardy said, "was that if you had to resort to war, have it
away from home."

Completely aside from such interests in defense and protection of homeland, there is another strong element in the
support of the war which might come under the general
heading of the American Christian Missionary Tradition, a
strain in the society that is connected with some of the nation's first expansion outside its own continent. It was not
any base political reason that motivated President McKinley
to annex the Philippine Islands in 1898, but rather a message
direct from God in which the Almighty told McKinley that it
was America's duty "to educate the Filipinos and uplift and
civilize and Christianize them, and by God's grace do the
very best we could by them, as our fellowmen for whom
Christ died."

UN Secretary General U Thant has spoken of the sense in
which the U.S. involvement in Vietnam seems to be a "Holy
War Against Communism," and if God has not directly
spoken this time to the President on the matter, the mission-

ary zeal has been a part of this as of all other wars engaged in by the United States. Shortly after President Johnson ordered the bombing of North Vietnam, he said in a speech at Catholic University that "what America has done, and what America is doing now around the world, draws from deep and flowing springs of moral duty, and let none underestimate the depth and flow of those wellsprings of American purpose."

The sense of moral and religious rather than political purpose for the war in Vietnam was articulated in a column called "The Chaplain's Corner," in the February, 1967, issue of *The Green Beret*, "a publication of the 5th Special Forces Group (Abn), Vietnam." The Reverend Charles J. McDonnell, Chaplain (CPT), U.S.A., wrote in an attempt to answer what was evidently a question troubling some of the men fighting in Vietnam: "Is It Worth It?" The Reverend McDonnell explained: "Why are we here? It is because God commands us to help our neighbor. He said, 'Whatever you do for these my children, you do for Me.' We are here because we love our families. We are here because it is where we belong. . . ."

Many citizens deeply believe that it is the duty of the country to spread its "way of life," as embodied in government as well as economics and religion, to less favored peoples of the earth. That is one reason why the holding of democratic elections in South Vietnam seemed terribly important as a justification back home for the U.S. involvement there, in spite of the fact that, as Senator Robert Kennedy pointed out, the victors received only 34 percent of the vote, from the roughly three fifths of the country not under Viet Cong control, and with no candidate allowed to run who was sympathetic to or even "neutral" toward the National Liberation Front, whose leaders as well as most of its members are South Vietnamese. No matter; the important thing, at least to the United States, was that South Vietnam was getting a form of government modeled after that of the United States. This was one of the prime accomplishments in what Vice President Humphrey has called America's program of "nation-building" in Vietnam.

The sincere belief that their country is bringing a better way of life to the Vietnamese people is one of the things that sustains many soldiers in their service there, and the evidence which they bitterly experience in the lack of appreciation or the hostility of many of the people can be justified by the fact that they don't know what's good for them, that their very opposition only proves the backward condition from which the Americans are engaged in uplifting them. James Lee Barrett, a talented young Hollywood screenwriter, went to Vietnam to gather material for writing a screen treatment of the John Wayne *Green Berets* movie, and among the many things that impressed him over there was the attitude expressed by one officer who told him that "these people don't want to be free, but by God, we're going to *make* them free!"

"To me," Barrett said, "that's a new and exciting concept."

While he was in Vietnam, Barrett was in areas of combat, and he found something else exciting which also seemed involved in the very reason for the war being fought. Barrett is an honest and intelligent man, and this factor he spoke of is something that is rarely if ever discussed or admitted, not because it isn't true but because it isn't popular or acceptable or even thinkable to most people, even those who may have experienced or felt it. "I tell you," Barrett said, "being over there in that kind of danger, where a grenade might get you while you're sleeping because there's usually some Vee Cee in every outfit, and the fighting and getting shot at, it's *exhila-*

rating. I really believe that men don't want peace. If they did, they'd have it. Men want war."

I later recalled this conversation when I heard the young civil rights defector at the SCLC conference in Atlanta use the same word—*exhilarating*—to describe the coming wars in the streets of the cities. This element of satisfaction, even relief, in violence and danger is always wrapped up in other rationalizations, which does not mean that the more polite and acceptable explanations for armed conflict at home and abroad are not also valid and sincere, but that this unmentionable factor is there too, a part of human behavior that men prefer not to think of as human.

The mission of *making* people free, of bringing to them by force, if necessary, a better way of life, is not only a sincere but also a justifiable motive to the believer, and this is an important factor to many of the men who serve in this particular war. Frank Naylor of Wichita, Kansas, served as a naval officer in Vietnam and is now chairman of the Vietnam Veterans Committee of the American Legion, and gives talks about the war at clubs and colleges and civic groups in his area. Naylor said many people in the States didn't have an understanding of the war, and he stressed that "most people don't realize how much the men over there do on their free time. Some of them work fourteen hours a day and then go to some village to help the people build new buildings, improve things, show them better methods of getting things done."

I asked if the men didn't get discouraged by the feeling that these efforts weren't always appreciated, that the people sometimes regarded them as intruders and enemies despite all their efforts, and Naylor said this indeed was occasionally discouraging.

"In other wars," he said, "the people fully supported us

when we liberated them, but that's not always true in this war. That makes things more difficult, because we have to get the people to appreciate the kind of government and the kind of life we're talking about. The people in the city are dependent on free enterprise, and so they know they've got something to lose if the Communists win, but in the country-side, where they've never known any other way of life, a lot of them have reached the point where a full stomach is their prime concern."

So in many cases the people must be mentally as well as militarily liberated. There is no doubt of the commitment and devotion of the many men who fight or work fourteen hours a day and then volunteer to help some village, and this phenomenon, this belief in the rightness of fighting in order to bring a better or "American" way of life to an often ungrateful population, indicates an interesting personality type that has been little recognized in the society of super-nation. All students of Americana are familiar with the much-maligned "do-gooder," the idealistic sort of person who wants to help his fellowmen, who grieves for the poor and downtrodden and devotes himself to the improvement of their condition. This "do-good" impulse, which often is ex-pressed domestically by service in settlement houses and fed-eral poverty projects and church work in the slums, was given an international outlet through the Peace Corps, which enabled the "do-gooders" to express themselves in for-eign lands and show by their own example that many Americans had the best interest of the other peoples of the world at heart. But surely it is this same principle that in a different sense drives those men who wish by military as well as social means to uplift the native, to enlighten the poor foreigner who doesn't even *want* to be free but has to be forced into that exalted condition. There are in America, unrecognized and unsung, devoted men of action and ideal-

ism who might be honestly described as "Hawk Do-Gooders."
They will make you free, even if it kills them (and you, too)
in the process.

---

iii. *The American Legion tries to recruit Vietnam veterans;
General Chieu gets a cap; veterans in East Harlem support the defense of the nation in spite of the injustices
of "Charlie Man"*

Is traditional patriotism becoming outmoded?

The question was raised by one of the speakers at the most
recent annual convention of the American Legion, an organization which has been a bastion of patriotism for half a
century, and which now is trying to change its image, partly
in an effort to appeal to the young returning veterans of
Vietnam. The Legion does not wish to change the patriotic
part of its image (except perhaps in the emphasis on the
organization's "military" nature, which seems to be a hin-
drance in attracting the younger veterans) but rather to play
down the "fun" part of its image, the reputation for being a
hard-drinking, high-living outfit, a rowdy band of middle-
aged conventioneers with water pistols and electric canes for
shocking other citizens—all in good fun.

At its forty-ninth annual convention last year the Legion
made what it calls its "encampment" in Boston, tenting at
the Sheraton-Boston Hotel, and convening en masse at the
city's new War Memorial Auditorium. The new sobriety of
the Legion's gatherings was literally brought home to me
when I went at cocktail time to visit the "hospitality suite"
of one of the two rival candidates for the presidency of the
organization. The "hospitality suite" is common to all con-
ventions in the U.S., and is usually a room or two taken by a
company outside the convening organization or a faction or

group within it which is promoting itself or its products, and as part of the solicitation of goodwill for its cause keeps a fairly continuous bar going, sometimes stocked with pleasant-looking hostesses who serve shrimp or pretzels to be munched while the booze is consumed. At the "hospitality suite" of the first presidential candidate (I don't know whose it was, as both candidates were named "Bill," with quotation marks, and each looked as identically firm-jawed and wholesome as the other in the big campaign posters in the lobby), there were three or four gray-haired Legionnaires, and a few wives, and a large punch bowl containing—pure fruit punch with no alcohol. I drank one cup of the stuff out of politeness, and said I must get on to the next hospitality suite. The only thing I could imagine was that the first candidate whose suite I had come to was running on a prohibition ticket, and had no chance at all, and so was not journalistically worthy of too much attention.

In the hospitality suite of the second "Bill" running for Legion president, I was greeted by pretty much the same scene, with a suspiciously similar looking bowl of punch containing—fruit punch with no alcohol. Downing my second fruit punch, I began talking with a gentleman who was a member of the East Orange (New Jersey) Post #73, and he told me something about the difficulties of recruiting veterans from the Vietnam War for the local Legion Post.

"There are none in my own Post," he said. "They're slow to come in—they come home, you go talk to them, they say 'Well, I don't want to wear a uniform anymore. Not right now anyway—maybe I'll come in later.' They don't want to be associated right away, I think because some of them feel the Legion is a 'military' organization."

As part of its program to attract the young Vietnam veterans, the Legion is attempting to offer them help in a variety of ways, with information about veterans' rights and benefits, and also any sort of aid that can be given while the men are still in service. The Post 73 man assured me this sort of help sometimes paid off, and he cited an example: "There's a nephew of a friend of mine who was blinded in Vietnam, and somehow while he was in the hospital his orders got lost and he couldn't get home. Well, I made inquiries, and got the whole thing straightened out for him. You can imagine he appreciated getting some help at a time like that—he was not only blinded but his face was partially shot away. He appreciated what I did, with the help of the Legion, and he wants to be a member. So here's a fellow, a Vietnam veteran, who's just waiting to get into the American Legion."

As well as such aid to individuals, the Legion conducts drives for the general welfare of the servicemen in Vietnam, as for instance one by the Legion's "Department of New Jersey" which collected $125,000 for gifts such as writing paper, cigarettes, and manicure items, which the Post 73 Legionnaire said were then flown over to Vietnam by the New Jersey National Guard. He said that before the New Jersey Drive had begun, his own East Orange Post had already started a drive of its own and collected eight hundred dollars.

"We were trying to decide how to best spend the money," he explained, "and someone got a happy idea from the TV comedy *F Troop*, which is about the military in the old West fighting the Indians. We thought we'd get in touch with a real F Troop in Vietnam and donate the money to their company fund. The trouble was, they didn't have any F Troop over there at the time—there had been one, but it had just been disbanded. Well, we inquired further then about worthy causes, and while we were trying to decide, we were asked to contribute to a building fund for a new chapel in Vietnam. It would be a permanent building, left there even after the war was over, so the people could use it even after the servicemen were gone. Well, that idea hit us right between the eyes. Everyone agreed to donate the money to the building fund for the chapel."

Escalation of programs to give Legion aid to the servicemen was urged at the convention in a "Report of the Vietnam Era Advisory Committee," made up of some of the veterans of Vietnam who had joined the American Legion and wished to help the organization recruit more men from their own young generation. Frank Naylor, the committee chairman, who had talked with me about some of the problems and the dedication he had seen among the men in Vietnam while serving there himself, also discussed some of the problems of recruiting the men for the Legion when they got back home. Naylor and I discussed these matters over drinks (not many, of course) in a hotel cocktail lounge, along with Mike Seis, a friend of Naylor's who had founded "First Vietnam Post 155" of Wichita, Kansas, the first Legion post made up entirely of "Vietnam Era" veterans.

Naylor said one of the problems of getting the young veterans involved in the Legion was that "our public image needs to get corrected. We want to make veterans aware of what the Legion does in youth work, rehabilitation, constructive programs like that. The public has no conception of what the Legion does in those fields."

Mike Seis agreed and said, "We're trying to live down the old impression of the Legion as a bunch of drunks. That idea hurts, let me tell you. I tried to sign up a young fella not long ago, and his wife told him 'Oh no, you're not gonna join a bunch of drunkards.' "

Another problem plaguing the Legion, as most other institutions in the society, is the "generation gap." The young men often didn't feel comfortable socializing with veterans of the World War II generation, the generation of their fathers. This was one of the reasons for Mike's founding the all-Vietnam Post, which brought together men who were all of the younger generation and shared common experiences and attitudes. While other such "young generation" posts would probably be formed, the Vietnam Veterans Committee had recommended that established posts attempt to attract new veterans, and suggested that "the local post develop young activities for its new generation, but in no instance should these activities be so limited in interest and scope that the entire post membership cannot actively participate and enjoy this phase of post activities."

This would seem to rule out rock 'n' roll dances, psychedelic light shows, and other forms of entertainment which might alienate as many older veterans as it attracted younger ones. It would certainly rule out "pot parties," even though marijuana smoking has become one of the more popular pastimes of soldiers in Vietnam. Although there have been many news stories reporting the incidence of marijuana use among servicemen in Vietnam, and many arrests for possession of pot, the drug is still associated almost exclusively with long-haired hippies in the public mind; crew-cut soldiers are simply not associated with marijuana use. Perhaps this is another indication of the generation gap; for *youth*, both longhair and crew-cut, draft-resister and combat soldier, share a predilection for a drug that is not approved of or understood or tolerated by most of the liquor-committed generation just above them.

The whole problem of finding activities which appeal to youth and yet which "the entire post membership" can participate in and enjoy is the real dilemma, and will surely be a challenge to every local Legion Post with a "mixed generation" membership. The recognition of the generation gap problem had in fact stirred the Legion to invite a young Vietnam era veteran from each of the states of the union to form the advisory committee which issued its recommendations to the convention at large.

The convention program had devoted two pages to the names and photographs of the members of this advisory committee, and I noticed that none of the forty-four shown in the layout were Negroes. It is true that there were six names which did not have accompanying photos, and simply had blank squares where the photos should be, and it was possible that any or all of these faceless committee members were Negroes. The last name under one of the missing pictures was Humble, a veteran identified as a post member from a southern state, and it seemed possible, for instance, that this was a Negro veteran of Vietnam who the Legion had sent to its convention, but there was no way of knowing for certain. Even so, it seemed odd that so few (if any) Negroes were represented among the veterans of a war in which so many Negroes serve and die, and I asked Naylor and Seis about this seeming discrepancy.

"A lot of your colored men reenlist," Seis explained. "The service of course is integrated, and in fact it's a model of integration for the rest of the country. I've personally gone out and signed up colored men—as they come back, I think the Legion will have a larger percentage from our Vietnam era than from any other war. This is really the first time there haven't been segregated units, and as a result of World War II there are some segregated Legion Posts. In Wichita, for instance, we have a colored Post. They prefer it that way—and let me tell you, that Post does a terrific job."

"That's right," Naylor said. "They do a good job, and if they want it that way—well, you can't legislate personal feelings."

✦ ✦ ✦

The American Legion Baseball program has been a great experience for me. With the aid of this program, I was able to develop my baseball abilities to the point that I received an athletic scholarship to the University of Alabama. This came even though I had not started for my local high school team in Tuscaloosa.

—*William Corbett Parker, Jr., 1967 American Legion Baseball Player of the Year*

✦ ✦ ✦

However great the problems of the American Legion in the new Vietnam Era, they must surely seem small beside the problems of the Vietnamese Veterans Legion, which had sent a small delegation to speak to veterans' groups in the U.S. in order to rally support for the often-critized South Vietnamese troops and hopefully to stir sympathy among fellow veterans. The Vietnamese group had appeared before the Veterans of Foreign Wars convention in New Orleans, the Amvets convention in Hollywood, Florida, and the Italian-American Veterans convention at Atlantic City, before coming to the American Legion convention in Boston. The Vietnamese delegation was headed by Lieutenant General Pham-Xuan Chieu, identified as the President of the Vietnamese Veterans Legion, and he was subjected to an American press conference with TV and newspaper reporters before addressing the main convention body of the American Legion.

In a private room off one of the corridors of the War Memorial auditorium, General Chieu, flanked by interpreters on either side (he gave his address in English, but wisely preferred further assistance for the press conference), was seated on a couch underneath a picture of John Collins, then Mayor of Boston. General Chieu, a small man with black hair slicked straight back, wore a black suit, white shirt, and black tie, and spoke in what was almost a whisper during the press conference.

After some preliminaries he was asked by a TV reporter: "How much confidence can we have in Marshall Ky, when a news story today reported that crowds in Vietnam booed him and taunted him, saying 'Down with the cowboy. Down with the hooligan'?"

General Chieu asked the newsman if he would repeat the question.

The newsman repeated the question, and General Chieu went into a huddle with his interpreters, and finally began responding to the question, speaking of responsibility and teamwork, and explaining that "there are charges against everybody who runs for office, as there are in all countries. The man who is elected will be elected by all the people, so he will have the support of all the people."

There were further explanations, and further discomforting questions, but most of the answers tried to indicate that things were pretty much the same over there as over here, "democracy-wise." The conference was called to a close by an American Legion official, and further proof of the similarity of the cultures of the two countries was offered before General Chieu and his entourage departed for the main convention hall, when they were given Vietnamese Veterans Legion caps to wear. The caps were blue and gold and looked very much like the caps of the American Legion itself. They had evidently been specially prepared for the occasion, since they were enclosed in cellophane wrappers that the Vietnamese Legionnaires had to tear open before setting the caps on their heads. Once the hats were adjusted and set at the proper angle, General Chieu and his fellow Legionnaires were led by their American Legion hosts through the auditorium corridors and display rooms toward the stage of the main hall. They had to pass through a large display area where many companies had set up booths advertising their products, and as I followed on the heels of the combined Vietnamese and American Legionnaires I thought it was a shame that the party didn't slow down so that the Vietnamese could have a closer look at some of the latest luxuries and amenities produced by a free, democratic society of the sort that was hopefully being built in their own country.

We passed a display of the Hammond Organ Studios of Boston, with a sign proclaiming "We Deliver Happiness," a booth operated by the New Hampshire State Lottery, a display of Jacuzzi whirlpool baths, and further on, the Niagara Cyclo-Massage, which tempted the citizen to "Enjoy Niagara's wonderful world of well-being." I slowed down to look at the displays but the Vietnamese Legionnaires were being hurried along, and I lost them somewhere around the exhibition of State Police Bloodhounds. There was a huge bloodhound, asleep in his cage, with a sign above him that said: "Bloodhounds such as these have performed countless errands of mercy for the Massachusetts State Police." Having lost the Vietnamese Legionnaires, I went to the refreshment counter and ordered a Schlitz and a hot dog, heavy on the mustard.

✦ ✦ ✦

NATIONAL SECURITY

The American Legion has always stood for a national defense strong enough to keep America free and peaceful. Hydrogen bombs, intercontinental missiles, and the conquest of space haven't changed the Legion's opinion.

—*"The Amazing Legion,"* a pamphlet published by the organization

✦ ✦ ✦

American veterans back from the war of course have their gripes, as soldiers do during and after all wars, but there seem to be a few different aspects this time about the complaints, things that are different from the sort of gripes common to an all-out war. There is of course resentment against the protesters and the lack of support at home, and also resentment about the government's direction of the war and the "limitations" on it. During the time of my travels, Secretary of Defense McNamara was cast in the image of the "Dove" within the war machinery, a civilian holding back the practical, hardheaded military men—or so the popular concept ran in the minds and talk of many soldiers as well as civilians. McNamara was the one man in government most often mentioned by veterans, usually in an unflattering way. On one occasion I asked permission to visit a military hospital, and the army public information man said it would be all right for me to come but asked that I not discuss "political questions" with the wounded veterans. "They're not politicians," he explained, "so don't ask them how they feel about McNamara or things like that."

The anti-McNamara sentiment was not only due to his "Dove" image but also to his symbolization of the much discussed modern methods of supplying the troops and developing armaments. When McNamara's departure from the Defense Department was announced, Joseph Alsop wrote a column extolling his great contribution in reorganizing the Pentagon operations on the "cost-effectiveness" basis he had learned in private industry. McNamara's innovations, said Alsop, had brought about a whole new way of "doing defense" (which used to be known as "waging war"). Ironically, though, some anti-McNamara veterans were hostile to the Secretary of Defense because of what they felt were the inefficiencies of his systems. One veteran complaining about lack of spare parts for arms and other equipment said, "You can't run the military like you can Ford Motor Company," which is how this sentiment had taken form, whether rightly or not.

In any war there are inefficiencies and complaints about arms and equipment, and yet ironically in this supposedly most "efficient" of all wars, there are gaffes and confusions that seem to the layman incredibly bizarre. With all the computers and efficiency studies and most modern of all arms development and perfection, complaints kept being registered about the most basic weapon of the foot soldier, the M-16 rifle. Soldiers in the field, disillusioned with its performance, hit upon the discovery that Dri-slide, put out by the Sears, Roebuck Company, was superior to the lubricant issued for the rifle by the army, and so the infantrymen began sending in to Sears, Roebuck with their own money and purchasing Dri-slide by mail order. To the soldier in some remote hamlet, waiting for the mail to see if his Dri-slide order had come from Sears, Roebuck that would enable him to fight with a more effective weapon, the grandiose "cost-effectiveness" of McNamara's revolutionary way of "doing defense" must have seemed bitterly remote, to say the least.

Aside from such logistic matters, there is confusion about the war itself, as illustrated by veterans like Pvt. Brown and sometimes justified by the "hawk do-gooder" rationale expressed by Frank Naylor and many others. A sense of the range of confusions and justifications of the men fighting the war can be glimpsed through an excellent collection of *Letters from Vietnam*, letters which servicemen wrote to their families and friends back home and which were sent in to *This Week* magazine and eventually published as a paperback book. There is often in the letters resentment about the lack of appreciation and cooperation from the people of South Vietnam, the sense that they "don't show any reason to warrant our help," as one soldier wrote. Yet the soldier found justification "from the political and moral-obligation aspect of it. While we're physically fighting the Viet Cong, we're politically fighting Communism. We're fighting, in particular, Red China and Russia. We've promised to help the Vietnamese win their war against the threat of Communism just as we've made our promise to the entire world to fight Communism . . ."

Some soldiers were appalled by the discovery that, as one put it after seeing an interrogation session carried out, "we use dirty methods too." The "guy from Intelligence" used a little electric "gadget" which produced shocks and burns on a woman being interrogated, and the soldier who witnessed it wrote:

> Then they took this same wire and tied it on the lady's husband and brother, but on their lower parts. I grabbed the damn thing and stuck it to the backass of the guy from Intelligence. . . . We wish we could send you a couple of those electrical gadgets to use on the powers that sent and keep us here. This must end soon or a lot of us will go nuts.

There is also expression in some of the letters of the first glimpses of doubt, as raised in the mind of a soldier writing to his folks about a patrol he had been on during the day: "We didn't run into any V.C., but we shot a couple of pigs, wrung a couple of chickens' necks, burned a house, and took some rice and peanuts. So we did OK and had a lot of fun. It suddenly dawned on me out there, 'Are we the good guys or the bad guys?' "

Naturally, the soldier risking his own life wishes to see himself and his sacrifice as part of the "good guy" cause, and it is often understood that way by those who come back and defend that way in discussions of the war—which must incidentally be another new aspect of this "limited conflict," for the veteran must come home not to flowers and praise, but often to questions and criticisms from his own friends and neighbors.

That's the way it was one evening in the East Harlem

neighborhood of New York City, where a friend of mine invited up to his apartment some of the men from the neighborhood who were veterans of Vietnam and some who had fought in World War II.

George and Joe, two Negro men who had fought in World War II, were debating the necessity of fighting in Vietnam. Joe was saying if we didn't fight far away like that the Communists would creep closer and they would build missile bases close to our own shores. George didn't agree insofar as China was the threat of such a development: "Don't worry about China," he said, "the sleeping dragon still sleeps."

Joe mentioned the loss of pride in the U.S., and the loss of prestige if it pulled out, but George countered that "France pulled out, why can't we?"

A few of the other half-dozen men commented back and forth as our host brought in some beer, and then George turned to a young Puerto Rican man from the neighborhood and said, "Al, you were there. Tell us what *you* think."

"When I went over," Al said, "I thought I had no business going over there. But I changed my mind. Our guys are getting killed, but they're getting killed with pride. You see they're helping those people, and I tell you, those poor people over there can't help themselves for nothin'. The people are ignorant, and they can't protect themselves. We saw the VC taking people by force—we tried to clear them out and help the people."

George said yes, but did the people seem to want this help, that's one thing he wondered about, and Al said, "You can't communicate with those people. That's the trouble. You go off, and then it starts all over again, the VC coming in."

Joe said he had a nephew over there, and, "My nephew says that's the trouble—he says you try to help the people and they turn around and kick you in the pants."

Al then pointed out the "military strategic" reason for

the war, which he felt was based on the fact that "if you don't stop Communism there, it's like a disease that keeps spreading."

Somebody challenged that, and Al backed down a little, saying that's just how he understood it but it better be true or there wasn't any use. "See, I'd fight for my home and family and friends—I'd fight to save each life right here in this room. But if I felt the war wasn't doing that, wasn't defending us back here, then I say it's all for nothing, and I say to hell with it."

Vic, another young man who had fought in Vietnam, mentioned some of the other confusing things about it.

"When I first got there," he said, "I was stationed on this rubber plantation south of Vietnam. One day I was fooling around and stuck my bayonet into this rubber tree, and it started bleeding, you know they bleed. The captain come up to me and he said, 'Hey soldier, that rubber tree belongs to the French, this is a French rubber plantation, and I better not see you messin' around or damagin' any of those rubber trees.' Well, after a while there, we got hit by the Cong, and when we started shooting back the fire hit some of the rubber trees and we let up a little 'cause of what the captain had said, but he come around and said what's wrong we're not firin' back enough and we tell him we don't want to hit the rubber trees, and man, that captain, he said *'Later for the rubber trees.'* So we didn't worry then, man, we just fired."

Vic said he also had seen some interrogation, and that you get used to it after a while.

"The sergeant he got suspicious of one of these girls who was hangin' around, and it turned out she had all our positions drawn on a map on her belly. The sergeant turned her over to the South Vietnamese and they interrogated her and I guess they beat her to death, that's the way it usually is. Then once we took five VC prisoners and they wouldn't talk, so the captain turned 'em over to the South Vietnamese and the South Vietnamese took 'em up in a helicopter. They took 'em I'd say about five thousand feet up and they kicked 'em out of the helicopter, one at a time, two of 'em were women. And man, that American captain he turned green and he heaved his brains out. I about laughed myself to death. You have to get used to it."

The question came up about why the U.S. should be doing all that stuff to the people over there, what about the situation at home for the black people, and the Puerto Ricans? The Negro men started exchanging stories of discrimination they had experienced after getting back from World War II, and one of them told about driving a truck and having to go through this small town in Texas where he couldn't get served any food and he had been on the road all day and was hungry.

"But I never forgot the name of that town," he said. "And you know what happened? A couple years later a hurricane came along and blew that town right off the map, I mean *destroyed* it."

There were other stories of "The Man" or "Mr. Charlie" or as he was called by one fellow "Charlie Man," the white oppressor, in his various lousy deals and tricks and keeping the black man down, but then the talk turned to the feeling that despite all this, it was probably better in the U.S. than anywhere else. It was worth fighting for, said the man who had passed through the Texas town that was later obliterated, and I asked how he could feel that way after recounting all the stories of discrimination he had experienced, and he said: "Well, we've got here the most powerful country in the world, and I guess you keep hoping it can change those things." Things like discrimination.

There seemed to be general agreement about this— everyone was willing to defend the country. The only ques-

tion was whether the war in Vietnam was essential to the
defense of the United States.

---

iv. *Even entertainment is limited in a time of limited war;
Mrs. Miller goes to entertain the troops; John Wayne
dons the Green Beret*

Jim Shelton is a former musician who works now for the
Hollywood Overseas Committee enlisting entertainers who
will volunteer to go to Vietnam as part of a USO show to
entertain the troops. Such recruitment is obviously a more
delicate and difficult task in controversial "limited wars" like
Vietnam than it is in popular, declared ones like World War
II, and Shelton explained that some entertainers feared that
if they went to Vietnam to entertain it would be taken as an
endorsement of the war itself. He said he tried to make it
clear to prospective volunteer performers that this was not
the case, and he often cited to them the philosophy of Danny
Kaye, who told Shelton that "the main thing is that you're
giving some pleasure to a group of young American boys,
and maybe they don't want to be there either, so the least
you can do is go and provide them some entertainment."

Although some performers were reluctant about going,
Shelton found that after they did they were always glad.
"Each person," he said, "has come back with a sort of re-
awakening of patriotic feelings, and a new appreciation of
our American heritage."

Mr. Shelton had come to the VIP lounge of the airport at
Los Angeles to give a briefing to the latest entertainment
troops bound for Vietnam, and I had met him there to hear
about the program and watch the embarkation of the show
as it set off for San Francisco and then Southeast Asia. This
particular show was billed as "Mrs. Miller and 'The Good

Guys,' with Edo Banto and Dori and Dave Robbins." Mrs. Miller, Shelton told me, had recently gained fame as "the singing grandmother," after being discovered as a member of the Foothill Drama and Choral Club of Claremont, California. "The Good Guys" were a pair of young fellows who sang along with Mrs. Miller, Dave and Dori were a husband-and-wife musical team, and Mr. Banto was listed in the program for the show as "an accordion virtuoso" who "has played at the leading hotels and night clubs across the country since 1932." The entire troupe gathered in a corner of the lounge, and Mr. Shelton was about to give his briefing when it was discovered that one of the "Good Guys" had forgotten to bring the medical certificate showing that he had the required vaccinations, and he rushed off to try to retrieve the card lest he be subjected to the shots all over again.

Shelton presented the certifiably vaccinated members of the troupe with a red, white and blue silk banner that said "The Mrs. Miller Show," khaki hats with a USO emblem, and pins that said "Spirit of '67." He briefed them on the fact that things were very expensive in Thailand, where they would be entertaining on part of their tour, but probably they wouldn't have to spend a nickel in Vietnam, the GI's were so appreciative of entertainers who came that they did everything for them.

Mrs. Miller, a plump lady in a brown knit dress, asked if she could visit an orphanage in Vietnam during her time off. Shelton said she could make that request but she must only do what her military hosts approved, for some things that might seem harmless could really be dangerous.

"Regrettably," he said, "the Oriental culture and heritage doesn't place value on human life, as we know it. There are cases where little children walk up to soldiers and are carrying bombs that explode, and everyone goes, even the child."

Shelton said they should just follow the advice of their

guides, and he assured them that "by the time you come back, your feeling of patriotism, and your feeling of our heritage will be renewed a thousand times over."

Just before departure time, the missing "Good Guy" returned with his vaccination certificate, and Shelton led the troupe out of the lounge and toward the plane. I hurried along, bringing up the rear with Edo Banto, the accordion virtuoso, and Dave Robbins, of the Dave and Dori team. Dave was a small, friendly guy who was lugging a large instrument that he said was an electric bass that he had bought especially for the tour. They boarded a commercial flight, but the stewardess had held the passenger line so that the troupe could board first, and they all seemed pleased with this VIP treatment. Jim and I waved good-bye. "The Mrs. Miller Show" was launched.

✦ ✦ ✦

The success of the Auburn Blood Drive came as no surprise to officials of Red Cross who are familiar with the tremendous spirit of the Auburn students. A hearty . . . WAR EAGLE ! !
— Salute, *magazine of the Birmingham area Red Cross*

✦ ✦ ✦

One of the most dramatic means of promoting home-front patriotism is the war movie—the action-packed picture which stirs sympathy for and confidence in the nation's troops as they battle the evil, wily enemy on land, sea, and air. World War II was the greatest war for movies, but even when that great war was over and the country took on a whole new set of enemies, there were "cold war movies" showing the intrigues of Russians as they brought the captive nations under the rule of godless Communism, and then there were Korean War movies, and then as the front of the cold war shifted to Asia, there were Chinese-Communist "anti-war-of-liberation" movies, showing the ruthless take-overs of small countries and the efforts of a handful of Americans to stop them, like Marlon Brando as the ambassador in *The Ugly American.* There was even a movie about the Berlin Airlift. To meet all of these challenges to the nation's security, Hollywood and the stars pitched in and made movies dramatizing the "human" as well as the political side of these new conflicts.

But there haven't been any movies about the war in Vietnam.

When John Wayne, a surefire box-office attraction whenever he puts on any sort of uniform and steps before the cameras, acquired the rights to the best-selling book about the war in Vietnam called *The Green Berets,* he had trouble finding a major studio that would contract to distribute the film. Batjac Productions, owned by Wayne, bought the rights to make *The Green Berets* into a movie, and after several refusals from major studios, found a distributor. The word in Hollywood was that the subject—the war in Vietnam—was "too controversial."

I went to see Wayne's son Michael in his office at Batjac Productions on the Paramount Studio lot in Hollywood to find out more about the origins and plans for the making of the first Vietnam War movie. Michael Wayne is an affable young man in his early thirties, and he greeted me from behind his desk where he sits in front of a rather sparsely furnished bookcase, whose volumes include *The Liberal Establishment* by M. Stanton Evans, *Prayer Can Change Your Life,* and *Who's Who In America.* I asked about the reluctance of Hollywood to make any movies about Vietnam, and Wayne bit off the end of a cigar, got up from his desk, and paced back and forth while he talked about the problems.

"There's some reticence in people's minds about the war—

about whether we should be there or not," he said. "I guess
in foreign countries they feel even stronger about whether
they like the U.S. being in Vietnam, and that's been one of
the reasons no one has done such a movie yet. The distribu-
tors are afraid the foreign grosses would be badly hurt, and
that's a big part of it. The foreign market has become increasingly important. For instance, in a John Wayne picture
today, fifty percent of the gross comes from the foreign market, while fifteen years ago it was only twenty-five percent."

Despite the potential handicap of the foreign reaction to a
movie about Vietnam, Michael Wayne felt that there were
many factors of positive appeal. "This war has not been exploited on the screen before," he said, "and the Green Berets
are a brand-new unit that's never been seen before. You see,
this is a war for men's minds, so these guys are trained not
just to kill but also to give medical aid, teach people how to
plant crops, provide sanitation—that's why they've been so
successful.

"Also there's a whole new type of military equipment used
in this war that hasn't been seen in movies—exotic new
weapons that are very interesting, very picturesque."

Wayne said that "the story we're doing won't be political,
but we do hope after people see it that they'll see we're doing
some good over there."

Mike Wayne had been to Vietnam himself to get the feel
of the place, and he was greatly impressed with the work that
the U.S. troops were doing there. He said it wasn't just a
matter of killing, but also of building, and he had been
particularly moved by the sight of the "Statues of Liberty
that our men have built in the villages." I said I hadn't
heard about this, and he buzzed for his secretary to bring in
some snapshots he had taken in Vietnam. He shuffled
through them and handed me a small photograph which
indeed showed a model replica of the Statue of Liberty,

standing in the middle of what seemed to be a little square in a small Vietnamese village. He said our men had built "hundreds" just like that, and I agreed it was certainly a unique accomplishment.

Going into the historical background of the conflict, Wayne said, "These people over there have been under the Chinese and under the French, but our troops are the first soldiers they really like. Who is it up in the North? Is it Ho Chi Minh, or is he the Chinese? No, he's the one in the North. He sent down two million terrorists who murdered every leader in South Vietnam. It was the same as if they'd come here and killed every senator, congressman, mayor, governor, everything. Then they were going to hold these elections, but of course they'd have been rigged, with all the real leaders murdered, so we stepped in and we're going to stay until they can have those elections.

"Dad was one of the first actors to go visit Vietnam," Michael said. "He felt it was his duty to go. He spent four or five weeks touring Special Forces camps, and visiting hospitals, and he got a real feeling for the people. The feeling of the people is fantastic—they gave Dad a Montagnard bracelet, and some brass things. Dad says the morale of our own troops is higher than in World War II or in Korea."

He smiled, and said, "Just to give you an example . . ."

He opened his desk drawer and pulled out a silver cigarette lighter that he said one of the men in Vietnam had given his dad. He handed me the lighter, and told me to read the inscription. It said "5th Special Forces Group."

"Now," said Wayne, "turn it over."

I turned the lighter over, and on the other side, engraved in large gold letters, was a two-word slogan. I looked up at Wayne, who was smiling his approval. The gold-lettered inscription said:

FUCK COMMUNISM

B. *The administration defends itself and tries to be patriotic — but not too patriotic*

The administration has set itself the difficult task of trying to maintain support for its war policy without stirring up too much emotional patriotic sentiment, but of course it must endorse and praise the patriotism of the men who fight and die. It must resist the arguments of patriots who wish to "win" the war by escalating further than the administration wishes to escalate at any particular time, and yet must not appear unpatriotic in this refusal. It is obvious that this is very complicated, and the President often expresses the wish that people would realize that the administration has access to more information than the public, and the public should trust its government to do the right thing. This attitude was critically appraised by the Washington *Star* as the "Daddy Knows Best" philosophy, and it is not acceptable to most of the press and the people. So the administration must meet the press and face the nation, and sometimes send its representatives into the countryside to try to explain things.

i. *The Vice President returns from Saigon and reports to the grocery manufacturers of America; in personal conversation he explains how "we catch hell both ways"*

The Vice President has served as one of the principal pleaders and salesmen of the administration policy, speaking and shaking hands and parrying questions with the well-known enthusiasm that he brings to all his tasks, a seemingly indefatigable campaigner whose pep and energy led one Washington reporter to describe him privately as "a natural cheerleader."

In his role as cheerleader for the Vietnam policy, Vice President Humphrey had gone on a mission to Saigon and other Southeast Asian capitals and returned to tell the public how well things were going. He made his first report on his findings at a luncheon meeting of the Grocery Manufacturers of America, who were convened at the Waldorf Astoria in New York.

I accompanied the Vice President and his party on this trip, and followed in the wake of the Humphrey entrance to the luncheon, which was marked by a rousing version of "Minnesota, Hats Off to Thee." Mr. Humphrey was led to the speakers' table on a stage overlooking the ballroom, and I made my way to a table in the audience with a few empty seats. The other guests at the table were lady grocery manufacturers with large swoopy hats, one of whom wondered why I wasn't eating. I explained that I had flown up from Washington with the Vice President's party, and we were served something on the plane. "I guess they were vice-presidential sandwiches," I said, and a pretty lady arched her eyebrows and said, "Really? What were they—baloney?"

This sort of hostility was not expressed by the majority of the audience when the Vice President gave his address, but neither was there great enthusiasm. The Vice President recounted all the different aspects of progress he had seen in Vietnam, but the listing of them did not produce any applause. The speech was only twice in forty or so minutes interrupted by applause, and then it was not unanimous, and at one point was almost requested, when Mr. Humphrey said he had assured the men in Vietnam that the "overwhelming majority" back home supported them. When there was no response, he said, "And I think you do," and then finally most of the audience joined in applause, but even some people at the speakers' table sat with folded hands.

What seemed to be the principal reaction to the report on the war was expressed by some of the grocery manufacturers who were talking among themselves at a reception for the Vice President following the speech. One manufacturer said, with a tone of resignation, "I guess what he said in there will be our policy for a while." A man standing beside him said, "Well, I agree with it. It's just like in business. You come to a certain point, you've invested so much, and you just can't back down. You've got to go ahead with it."

Back aboard Air Force Two, the sleek silver Jetstar that carries the Vice President on most of his government duties in the United States, Mr. Humphrey stretched, looked out at the panoramic view of Manhattan below, and said, "That's really a sight for a country boy like me."

On one of the Jetstar trips I sat in the back compartment which has two facing seats on each side of the aisle, with a collapsible table that can be set up between the seats for dining or looking over papers and notes. I wrote in my notebook on this table while the Vice President answered questions with interest and enthusiasm, occasionally looking across at what I was writing and pointing to some statement or figure he wished to emphasize.

I asked what he felt the reasons were for the widespread dissent about the war, and he began by citing the influence of television, saying that this was "the first time people have seen a real war, live, in their living room."

He also placed emphasis on the generation gap. "This new young generation has never known a depression or a war, and it hasn't learned about these things from hard experience," he said.

The young-generation phenomenon, Mr. Humphrey felt, "isn't just limited to antiwar feeling about Vietnam. It's a more general kind of self-indulgence. And it isn't limited to young people in America; it's also true of young people in Europe."

In his speech to the grocery manufacturers, Mr. Humphrey had said "as an old dissenter" he was not opposed to dissent, but asked those who dissented to consider the effects on the men fighting in the war, and the possible effects on the morale of the enemy as well as of our own troops. I asked him what he felt were the proper limits of dissent, or ways of expressing it, and he said: "We have a permissive society, and dissent is part of our education. But I don't see how you can have an organized society if, for instance, the citizen can decide he won't pay taxes for the war, or for any other policy he doesn't like. When I lived in Minneapolis, I paid taxes for things I didn't like at all, but if you're going to have a government, the citizen has to pay his taxes."

I asked about the draft resisters, and Mr. Humphrey said, "I have respect for young men who are real C.O.'s, who are opposed to all wars because of killing and the cruelty of war, but I don't respect a guy who says he will fight, for instance, in India, but he won't fight in Vietnam."

I asked about the criticism from older people, intellectuals and former government men who surely did not criticize the war because of "generation" misunderstanding. The VP said, "Well, part of that criticism is just anti-Johnson. But some of it is based on a sincere belief that we ought not to be in this war, and they are able to put up a pretty good case."

"I think we've got to be careful," he said, "not to dampen dissent because we don't like what people are saying. As long as they give the other fellow a chance to be heard. Now, the ones who just holler and walk out and won't listen to the government's position, they're just hooligans."

Mr. Humphrey seems much less rigid on those matters when discussing them in conversation than he does in his speeches, which include some of the administration's hottest attacks against dissenters. Also his appraisal of the Vietnam situation is less rigid in conversation than in the rhetoric of public oratory. Before the grocery manufacturers he had said that the enemy in Vietnam was not "a bunch of indigenous Robin Hoods," and emphasized the necessity of halting Communist aggression. A listener might have drawn the inference—in fact, a belief widely held in the United States—that all of the U.S. opponents in Vietnam were Communists, and that a lot of them weren't even Vietnamese (not being "indigenous"). In our conversation, however, while expressing his belief that "the NLF is a creation of Hanoi," Mr. Humphrey said, "There's no doubt that there are non-Communist elements in the Viet Cong. There are some strong nationalist elements, people who are just unhappy with things in their country and have been unhappy for a long time."

I asked Mr. Humphrey how he answered the dissenters who urged an enlargement of the war rather than a withdrawal from it, those patriots like Donald Lobsinger who couldn't understand why the nation was fighting Communism and at the same time giving aid to some Communist nations and trading with Communist nations.

The Vice President nodded, and said he knew that this was a difficult thing for people to understand. "We see this war in Vietnam not as a great war," he said, "but as a struggle with Communism in a limited area. We're trying to confine the struggle to that one area, and at the same time, by using restraint, we're trying to carry on normal relations with the rest of the world."

Mr. Humphrey pointed out that while many conservatives

wanted the government to decrease its spending and efforts in the war on poverty and escalate the war in Vietnam, on the other hand many liberals wanted the government to spend less on the war in Vietnam and much more in the war on poverty. "So you see," he said, "we catch hell both ways."

Despite these problems, the Vice President was not altogether discouraged about the state of the nation, and in fact felt that much of the unrest and dissent was an indication of the deep changes through which the society was moving.

"We're moving out of segregation and discrimination in race to an era of real equality. We're moving to attack the roots of poverty, to eliminate it altogether, and that's as great a change as the move from the mercantile system to the industrial system. It's like what happens in an airplane—when you have a period of turbulence in passing from a high pressure area to a low pressure area. That's inevitable. I think twenty years from now we may look back on this time and be amazed that there wasn't more turbulence than there is."

---

ii. *The Secretary of State reveals that as a young man he picketed against sending scrap metal to Japan*

The Department of State is housed in a large white building that might be mistaken for a hospital. Inside the glass doors of the main entrance, a uniformed guard at an oval desk checks credentials, and the visitor who is admitted passes into a vast, anonymous lobby and then boards an elevator. The office of the Secretary of State is itself large and austere, featuring a mammoth desk. Across the desk on the other side of the room is a couch flanked by two chairs, and when I visited the Secretary he invited me to take a seat there, and came over himself to converse in that slightly less formal situation than a confrontation across his giant desk.

Secretary of State Dean Rusk is a tall, balding man with something of the aura of a headmaster who has dealt with many sensitive problems and handled them all to the satisfaction of the board of trustees. If some men in public life are said to "exude" a certain quality, such as charm, or enthusiasm, or militance, it might be said that Dean Rusk exudes . . . composure.

Discussing the reasons for the antiwar sentiment in the nation, the Secretary said that "part of it is television. For the first time, people see the war on TV, right in their own living room."

He also feels that television as well as other media of information "are more accessible to protesters." "I can give a lecture, as I did recently, with 14,000 people in the audience, and if there are three people with a picket sign in the audience, they are singled out by the TV cameras. In this particular case, in the television coverage, I got 'equal time' with the picket sign."

Secretary Rusk said he was certainly not against dissent, or demonstrations, "as long as they aren't trying to take the platform away from you, using tactics like storm troopers." Demonstrations and picketing were certainly not wrong in themselves, and in fact Secretary Rusk said, "When I was young, I participated in demonstrations myself. I picketed against sending scrap iron to Japan before World War II."

He said he felt another reason for the antiwar feeling being greater and more apparent now than during the Korean War was that "there is a much more organized effort by the Communist 'Apparatus' on a worldwide scale."

He said he didn't mean to imply that all the people who participated in demonstrations were Communists, but that the work of the Communists "explains some of the hard-core protest, demonstrations where real incidents occur."

In addition to television and Communism, the Secretary said he felt the protest against the war was also, in part, due to the "generation gap."

"World War II is twenty years away now, and World War I was twenty years before that. A lot of years, and a lot of answers get forgotten. And some people now aren't old enough to even remember them. I have to pinch myself to realize that young people who are freshmen and sophomores in high school now were only six years old when I became Secretary of State.

"The young people who haven't experienced any other war feel that the war in Vietnam is something that is all fresh and different, that it has nothing to do with other crises. A lot of arguments I hear now against the war are the same ones people used in the thirties, the same sort of things people said to me in the thirties in arguing against arming or preparing for a war against Germany."

It could be, the Secretary said, that the country today was undergoing a great cyclical change, back to isolationism. But he felt that if that was what they wanted, if they wanted to change the course of the nation's policy, it should be done and would be done through national elections.

Despite the vociferous protest and complaints about the war, both from those who wished to end it and those who wished to escalate it further, Seecretary Rusk felt that neither of these positions represented a significant feeling among the populace at large. There were disagreements about policy, about the way of conducting the war, the Secretary felt, but "there we're talking about a middle part of the spectrum, in a national sense."

As the situation looks from his vantage point in the State

Department, "We don't see any real pressure to pull out or to have a bigger war."

Conclusion: In the face of great domestic controversy on the nation's foreign policy, the Secretary of State has not lost his composure.

✦ ✦ ✦

A FLASHBACK

It was midnight in Manhattan, Sunday, April 16, when the telephone rang in the fashionable East Side apartment of Lem Jones. Sleepily, Jones answered, then came alert with a jolt. It was the Central Intelligence Agency calling from Washington.

"This is it," Jones' Agency contact told him. The invasion had begun. The CIA man dictated the first communique, to be issued to the world by Jones in the name of the Cuban Revolutionary Council. Jones took it down in longhand on a pad.

"Before dawn," the CIA man dictated slowly, "Cuban patriots in the cities and in the hills began the battle to liberate our homeland from the despotic rule of Fidel Castro and rid Cuba of international Communism's cruel oppression. . . ."

—*The Invisible Government,*
by David Wise and Thomas B. Ross

✦ ✦ ✦

Just as Washington, in the sense that the city means "the government," is a kind of illusion to the rest of the country, a place about which one reads and hears rumors and which seems essentially too complicated and mysterious to understand, so in all those aspects the rest of the country seems an illusion to Washington. And just as the citizen may finally decide the best thing is to assume that despite all that the critics and the pundits and prophets of doom may say, the government is really not too far out of line, so official Washington may come to adopt a similar conclusion about the country.

If many disturbing things seem to be going on in the country, well, these things cannot be denied by Washington, but they can be explained—explained in a way that makes them seem not really relevant, not really an indication that Washington is pursuing the wrong policy, even though it may be unpopular among some elements. Take the war in Vietnam, which has stirred more protest and discontent than any war in at least a century. The government cannot deny this but it can explain it by such factors as Television, the Generation Gap, and sometimes, the Communist Apparatus. It is significant that these explanations have nothing to do with the possible validity of the opposition, and in fact not only avoid that matter but discount it by the nature of the explanations.

Washington does what it thinks is best for the country, just as parents do for their children, and like a hardworking parent who has worked and slaved and sacrificed and is not appreciated by the children, so Washington is hurt and feels misunderstood when the country doesn't love it. From time to time the President invites a small number of reporters in to talk informally and off the record in what is called a "backgrounder," and reporters who have attended say the President gets especially upset about how the press emphasizes the negative things and doesn't talk about all the good things the government has done. The President names many of the good things, and then in mock seriousness says to the reporters, please don't mention those things, those things are a secret. The President's staff has prepared him a memo about how all Presidents are criticized during a war, and how most wars are unpopular, and the President read this rather lengthy document to one group of reporters at a backgrounder, going from George Washington to himself, and including even Buchanan, who is not much remembered for anything, much less that he suffered criticism during a war.

The outsiders seldom understand, and being in high government position is indeed an inside phenomenon, with one of the strongest mystiques of any in the world, sustained and strengthened by the feeling of power; and men are as unlikely to give up power once they have had a taste of it as they are to give up sex after having had a taste of it.

James Thomson, who served in government, in the White House and in the State Department, under Presidents Kennedy and Johnson speaks of what he calls "the effectiveness trap" for men in government:

"This is the trap that keeps men from speaking out, as clearly or as often as they might, within the government; and it is the trap that keeps men from resigning in protest and airing their dissent outside the government. The inclination to remain silent or to acquiesce in the presence of the great men—to live to fight another day, to give on this issue so that you can be 'effective' on later issues—is overwhelming."

To lose one's effectiveness is of course to lose one's power, or one's contact with it.

This is not just at the highest levels, but it comes to most men who get a taste of it. I felt it in a young man who served on the staff of an important administration official, and who said that in his boss's realm, he was responsible for staying close to developments in Africa and Southeast Asia, or as he explained it, "I have the unwashed part of the world." I asked how he happened to "get" this part of the world for his work, and he said he had wanted it, it wasn't by accident, he had arranged it; or as he put it, "I architected it."

We talked about Vietnam, and he admitted there had been

many miscalculations. He admitted, as had President Eisenhower, that at the time of the French withdrawal from the country, Ho Chi Minh was the principal political hero in Vietnam, South as well as North (divisions created as a temporary expedient by the Geneva agreements), and that the United States hoped to build up a popular government in the South by aid to Diem and his followers. Despite advances and reforms made by Diem and the governments succeeding his, the administrator said that the popular support of a majority of the people had not yet been gained, and it was probably unwise for the United States to make major commitments of troops in a situation where such support did not exist to begin with. Having made the commitment, the United States, of course, had to stick with it, the young man felt. However, he speculated that the Vietnamese experience had been a "lesson" in this sense, and that the United States would not again make a major troop commitment in a situation in which popular support did not initially exist. Therefore, if only in this educational aspect, he felt that the Vietnam experience had been useful.

These were things that never would be said in public, for the public would not understand. As the President has often explained, in asking people to think before they dissent, the government has access to information that the public does not.

C. Young men are trained for limited war; death is within the limits

i. Counterinsurgency enters the high school ROTC curriculum; Mao is not consulted

In the corridors of Shortridge High School in Indianapolis was an assortment of homemade "recruiting" posters urging students to join the Reserve Officers Training Corps, a program offered in secondary schools and colleges throughout the nation which gives male students academic credit as well as preparation for a commission in the armed services upon college graduation. The posters in the corridors at Shortridge at the beginning of the fall semester bore slogans such as "Feel the Draft Coming On? Sign Up for ROTC," and "If You Have to Go, Be in the Know."

These were appeals not so much to the patriotism of the students as to their personal interest, a theme which fits in with the prevailing approach to such matters throughout the nation. I asked the director of the school's ROTC program if the Vietnam War had in any way helped stir recruitment for his corps, and he said, "What helped us most was when we explained to the students that joining the ROTC didn't mean they'd be drafted. A lot of them thought if they joined, they would have to go right in the army after high school graduation, and we explained that this wasn't the case at all.

In fact, as long as they're in the ROTC they're not subject to the draft. Now they understand that it will help them when they have to go in the service, when they get out of college. If you have four years of ROTC in high school, then you only have to have two years instead of the full four in college to get a commission when you graduate."

The fall recruitment drive had just barely saved the unit at Shortridge from extinction, for the U.S. Army, which re-imburses the local school boards for the salaries of the pro-gram's instructors through the Army retirement plan, re-quires a minimum of 100 students enrolled in the corps of each school. In the past academic year the Shortridge unit had only 88 members, and would have been dissolved if more than the 100 minimum weren't enrolled for the current year. In the face of this threat of extinction, the special "recruiting campaign" was launched, featuring the posters in the corri-dors, stories in the school paper, and a talk to the student body by the principal urging boys to take the course and enumerating the benefits it offered. In addition to all this, the director of the program said that "perhaps most impor-tant of all was the aid of Mrs. Horowitz, the mother of Cadet Captain Stephen Horowitz, a senior who is executive officer [the highest-ranking cadet] in the unit this year. Mrs. Hor-owitz talked to students and also talked with the mothers of students, and this helped a great deal."

As a result of all these efforts, spearheaded by the mother of Cadet Captain Horowitz, the unit was able to enlist 110 students out of an approximate male enrollment of 1,400 in the school and "hoped for 135" before the final closing of class schedules.

Master Sergeant Jerome Baker, who heads the ROTC pro-gram at Shortridge, said he had taught the course before in the Chicago public school system, where the enrollment minimum was not such a problem because "it's compulsory in the Chicago high schools for boys to take either ROTC or gym, and so you always have a good enrollment. You always get two hundred to three hundred students, as there are always some who prefer ROTC to running around a track or throwing a ball around."

In Indianapolis, where the course is voluntary, Sergeant Baker said that the biggest high school in the city had the largest unit: 300 students out of a male enrollment of roughly 2,500.

While I was talking with Sergeant Baker the class bell rang, and a dozen students had assembled in the ROTC classroom. The Sergeant said they would have drill today, and he instructed Cadet Captain Clarence Hudson to march the men outside to the football practice field alongside the school building. It was early in the semester, and the men had not been issued their uniforms yet, so Cadet Captain Hudson faced a unit that must have been as motley in appearance as the home militiamen that George Washington once had to whip into shape. Undisturbed, however, by either his shaggy troops or the squeals of a girls' gym class that was being held about fifty yards away, Cadet Captain Hudson conducted his instructions with dignity, putting the unit through basic drills and then testing their knowledge of military technicalities such as "What are the freedoms of the position at ease? Who can define the position of attention?"

I stood off to the side with Sergeant Baker, who explained to me that the ROTC program included not only drill instruction but map reading, the military code of conduct, respect for the flag, and military history from the American Revolutionary War to Vietnam. He said beginning this year there would also be a course in "Counterinsurgency." I asked if Mao Tse-tung's writing on guerrilla warfare would be used, and he laughed and said, no, "the U.S. has developed its own materials, based on the experience of the Rangers and the Special Forces. Naturally, the course in counter-insurgency will mainly be theory," he explained. "I mean, we can't have a kid injured by someone jumping out of a tree on him."

When I asked about his own army career, Sergeant Baker, a pleasant and very modest man, mentioned only that he had fought in Korea and was captured and held prisoner for twenty-seven and a half months. It was almost time for the class to end, and I walked back into the building with Sergeant Baker, following Cadet Captain Hudson's marching troops. It was a bright, warm autumn afternoon, squeals were still coming from the girls' gym class, and such things as imprisonment and counterinsurgency seemed terribly remote. In a way they were, and in a way they were not at all.

✦   ✦   ✦

VIETNAM'S WAR-RAVAGED CHILDREN

. . . How would you like it if one of your children came crawling into the house covered with blood, screaming in pain: "I was hit by a hand grenade, Mommy"?

. . . It is estimated that one million Vietnamese children have been wounded in this war. More than a quarter of a million children have been killed.

— Look, *April 18, 1967*

✦   ✦   ✦

ii. *A cordon and search mission is staged at a Vietnamese village in Virginia*

The village of Lang Suon Doi, with its thatch-roofed huts, its idle peasants, and its flagpole flying the colors of the

National Liberation Front, looked serene and safe beneath the cloudless sky. But then, all at once, the silence was shattered by the rattle of machine guns, the snap of rifle fire, and the deeper pounding of artillery. Clouds of smoke, pink and white and gray, puffed out of the surrounding landscape, and after the crescendo of sound had subsided, a deep voice announced through a loudspeaker system: "Welcome to Fort Belvoir's version of that colorful land, infested with Vee-Cee—South Vietnam!"

There was laughter and some scattered cheers and whistles from the wooden bleachers where several hundred young men in the khaki garb of the United States Army, some wearing black helmets with the insignia of Officers Candidate School, had been assembled for an afternoon of instruction concerning the type of guerrilla warfare they would encounter when they went to fight in Vietnam. The bleachers were set up on a hill that overlooked the simulated Vietnamese village, where lessons of ambush, patrol, and "counterinsurgency" were acted out in a sort of pantomime accompanied by an instructional narrative from officers who had served in Vietnam.

Major Bagdonas and Captain Quantock narrated a lesson on "ambush" in which a humorous, inept squad showed how *not* to go on patrol, and were all mowed down, while an efficient, serious squad showed how to do it right, and all survived. After the ambush lesson there was a coffee break and Major Bagdonas explained that this program of instruction had been going on for the past year, and that there were other "Vietnamese villages" at other army bases throughout the country, similar to the one here at Fort Belvoir, Virginia.

After the coffee break, Lieutenant Ellis of the artillery was master of ceremonies for the staging of one type of counterinsurgency, the "cordon and search" of an unfriendly village.

The Lieutenant explained that the villages in Vietnam were basically divided into three different types: (1) friendly toward us, (2) friendly toward us but controlled predominantly by guerrillas, and (3) nonfriendly toward us and controlled predominantly by guerrillas. It was important, he said, to determine beforehand which kind of village was being approached, because "we don't want to go in firing and shooting up a friendly village."

The demonstration about to take place in the simulated village below, however, was an example of a cordon and search operation in an unfriendly village. This had been determined by an advance patrol, and the Lieutenant explained that "it didn't take too much smarts for them to figure out this was an unfriendly village. For one thing, the Vee-Cee flag was flying from the village flagpole, and on the village bulletin board were pictures of May-O and Ho Chi Minh."

Having established the hostile nature of the village, the U.S. patrol surrounded it, stationing gunners on the ridge overlooking it, and out of the woods came soldiers moving stealthily toward the main gate. In the meantime, the villagers themselves (played by soldiers and WAC's wearing levis and old clothes) had seen the approaching troops and were scrambling around under the instructions of their "chief," who was identified by a big straw coolie-style hat, and immediately established himself as a comic character to the audience. It was well that the advancing troops moved stealthily, for they discovered the main gate to the village was booby-trapped, and demolition experts set off the bomb while the soldiers lay flat and safely on the ground. Once inside the village the different "teams" of the U.S. patrol went into action.

The "population control team" took the villagers over to

one corner, where they were searched for weapons and then questioned by the "interrogation team" for information. In the meantime, the "search team" was going into each hut, accompanied by the chief (who kept bowing and shuffling and getting a lot of laughs) as well as the head of the family, or "Papa-San," so that "we can't be accused of looting." In one house, the search team found some weapons, and in another hut some "documents." The Lieutenant explained that "for all we know, they could be any kind of documents —but they could be helpful to us." In the third hut, the search team found an actual live Vee-Cee, who shot one of the soldiers and tried to escape, but was shot himself. The soldier was only wounded, but the Vee-Cee was killed. Another Vee-Cee was discovered hiding in a tunnel, and so the "Mighty Mite" was called in. The Lieutenant explained that the Mighty Mite was a machine that poured gas into the tunnel, thus forcing out any Vee-Cee who might be hiding in it.

After these incidents, the civic action team went around giving out soap and candy, and medical supplies for "sores and colds." The psychological team took down the pictures of May-O and Ho from the bulletin board and put up "literature that we hope will encourage the people to come over to our side."

There was some quiet groaning and snickering from the troops sitting behind me in the bleachers, and one guy said, "Yeah, they're probably putting up a picture of LBJ." Another guy laughed and said, "Sure, that'll do it." There was some more snickering and someone said "Shee-it."

The process of pacifying the village was completed with the U.S. soldiers taking down the Vee-Cee flag and putting up a flag of the government of South Vietnam, which one of the psychological team had brought along for just such an occasion. "Now," said the Lieutenant, "the job is complete—they have converted this from a Vee-Cee village to a predominantly friendly village."

It seemed awfully simple, not only to me but to many of the men in the bleachers behind me. Beneath the groans, there were loudly whispered comments like "Ka-rist," and "shee-it," and after one cynical snort one soldier said, "Yeh—and then they lived happily ever after."

✦ ✦ ✦

> . . . In my 56 years in the Army, I have never seen better fed men, in peace or war. Ninety percent of the meals served to American personnel are hot. It is commonplace, according to some men I talked with, to have a helicopter hover over an embattled unit and lower what my wife termed "a businessman's breakfast" — fruit juice, two soft-boiled eggs, buttered toast, marmalade and hot coffee.
> — *"My Visit to Vietnam," by General Omar N. Bradley*, Look, *December 14, 1967*

✦ ✦ ✦

---

iii. *Cookies and comfort await the soldiers who pass through "the revolving door to war"*

The USO lounge at the San Francisco International Airport was labeled "Our Revolving Door to War" by the Burlingame (California) *Advance Star,* and through it go many of the troops on their way to and from Southeast Asia. In charge is Mrs. Evelyn Marks, an attractive brunette lady who is a veteran at organizing charity and volunteer programs for hospitals. The "limited war" and its attendant controversies have made difficulties for Mrs. Marks, and she said that in her own efforts to bring entertainment and publicity to the lounge, "We stress that we're not saying the war is right or wrong—we just say, well, the boys have to do it, so we try to be nice and make it easier for them. On that basis, we try to enlist the help of people, whatever they think about the war itself."

Mrs. Marks found that similar explanations were sometimes necessary in her own social life, when people learned of her work at the USO lounge and interpreted it as an endorsement of the war. "I'm very unpopular at dinner parties," she said. "I don't know anyone who is *for* the war, but since it's going on, someone has to help the boys."

This was indeed a new kind of wartime atmosphere, Mrs. Marks acknowledged. "I grew up in a flag-waving war, World War II," she said. "These boys today have it doubly hard because they're not getting that kind of public support. I tell the boys, 'Every generation has its war, and it just so happens your generation has an unpopular one!'"

Despite the unpopularity of the war, Mrs. Marks had been successful in gathering support for the boys and the lounge that serves them. She said that last Christmas a disc jockey named Jack Carney had started a "cookie-lift campaign," and all over the area, schools and churches had "cookie drives," and helicopters picked up the cookies and brought them to the lounge. So great was the response, in fact, that Mrs. Marks said, "We had to store thousands of pounds of cookies."

Performers who passed through had always come back enthusiastic, she said, even though they might have been reluctant at first: "You know, when they get to Vietnam, it's 'wall-to-wall' Americans over there, and they feel right at home. Efrem Zimbalist, Jr., told me he was 'lukewarm' about the war before going over, but 'red hot' when he got back. As Bob Hope said, 'You can't look at that sea of faces over there appreciating what you're doing for them, and not be moved by it.' "

There was satisfaction for Mrs. Marks too in seeing the boys and seeing some of the good effects the service has on them. "We get a lot of recruits who come in on their way to basic training," she said. "You know, they come in sloppy and with long hair and what have you. And when they come back after basic their backs are straight and it's, 'Yes, sir,' and 'Yes, Ma'am'—the transformation is marvelous. I said to one colonel, 'How do you do such a wonderful job with them?' and he smiled and said, 'It takes us eight weeks to do what the parents couldn't do in eighteen years.' "

Mrs. Marks said the boys not only came back in better condition from basic training, but also from Vietnam.

"They look so good when they come back. Before going over they look apprehensive. When they look that way, we try to introduce them to some boys who have already been over, and get them chatting. When they see these boys who've come out of it and are well and whole, it makes them feel much better. When they're waiting here before going over, it's as if they're sitting in a doctor's office. They need to be reassured."

Two men wandered in looking slightly lost, and Mrs. Marks jumped up and greeted them with "Hi, Soldier!" and got some cookies and coffee for them. Both had been in Vietnam, and one who said in a drawl that he came from West Virginia mentioned that he had signed up to go back over. Mrs. Marks looked to see if I was listening, and then she asked him why he was going back, and he said, "Well, I have a good job over there, and the pay is real good." Mrs. Marks came back to where I was sitting and whispered, "Did you

hear that? People don't believe that the boys want to go
back, but you just heard it—they do."

✦ ✦ ✦

HONORARY SKINNY DRAGON BRIEFS SAILORS ON DUTY IN THE PACIFIC

"You know what I'm gonna tell you
guys!" he shouted. "I'm not gonna tell
you not to pick up girls. I'm gonna
show you how! I'm gonna shock you
guys. I'm gonna give you a dose of
cultural shock," and throws out advice
that could keep many a young sailor
out of trouble, advice Dave says it took
him nearly decades to acquire. . . .

Dave's title is: "Head, Area Orienta-
tion Section, General Military Training
Branch, Education and Training Division of the Bureau of Naval Personnel."

— the Washington Star, November
13, 1967

✦ ✦ ✦

iv. *The nation honors those who die in its service; more
room is needed to bury them*

Small, oblong, olive-drab military buses waited at the gate
of Arlington National Cemetery and carried men, women,
and children up the winding road to the small amphitheater
where the Veterans Day ceremonies would be held in honor
of those who died in the nation's wars. The citizens who
came were mostly middle-aged or older, except for little children who came as part of families. The children were well
scrubbed and dressed as if for Sunday school, and there was
some of the feeling of going to church but also a kind of
holiday atmosphere, partly provided by the fun of riding up
the hill in the little buses.

Dignitaries of different veterans' organizations and of the federal government sat on the open stage, and to the side of these honored guests six torches, representing freedom, burned with small orange flames and thick black smoke that rose and drifted in the autumn air.

The Honorable Paul H. Nitze, Deputy Secretary of Defense, delivered the main address, as the personal representative of the President. He spoke in a tone of reverence and respect for those who served their country and who "sleep beneath these grassy slopes."

"It is not they who are unknown but we—they are known for what they did, for why they died. We have yet to prove how we shall serve. Shall we live for others as they did? Shall we do our onerous duty as they did?

"There are thousands who lie here as there are hundreds of thousands who lie across the nation and the globe. . . .

"There is littered on history's shore many a shipwrecked state. . . . The Romans said, 'If you want peace, prepare for war.' Yet Rome came to neglect that rule. . . .

"We see freedom as a flame—that is why we bear torches. It must be fueled—with our sacrifices, with our resolve.

"There are those who cannot distinguish between dissent and divisiveness. The totalitarian temptation is to read dissent as a disloyalty to duty. There *is* a divergence of views and may there always be. . . . But let those who would be our adversaries abroad inspect our ledger of loyalty. This Republic is ready to meet its responsibility, cost what it may."

The Navy Sea Chanters sang an anthem called "Once to Every Man and Nation," and then the Reverend Harold B. Fay, National Chaplain of the Veterans of World War I of the United States, delivered the Benediction, asking God to "bless our nation until the end of time. . . . We ask in the name of Thy son and our savior, Jesus Christ, our Lord."

Men and women bearing flags of different veterans' groups

marched down the center aisle and out of the amphitheater, while the U.S. Navy Band played "It's a Grand Old Flag."

They marched out onto a grassy slope, and then broke ranks, some folding their flags and some still holding them unfurled while snapshots were taken by friends. The flags were of mauve and orange, of gold and blue; of green and scarlet and cream and purple. There was one that said: "Ellen Spencer Tent #1, Daughters of Union Veterans, 1861-65," and others that said: "Wac Vets," "Gold Star Mothers of America," "George Mason Chapter of the Sons of the American Revolution." There was an old straight-backed man wearing a broad-brimmed hat and holding a flag that said "Spanish War Veterans," and there were two gray-haired ladies, one with an American flag and one with a flag that said: "Widows of World War I," and they wore gold capes that billowed behind them as they walked across the slope, bearing their banners.

The colors of the flags were joined by the colors of the season, and the vivid air was swept with dry leaves of burnt gold and brown and scarlet, floating and coming to rest across the hills that bore the small white identical markers of the graves, row on row, lining the quiet landscape as far as the eye could see—graves, graves, graves.

The cemetery, in fact, is nearly filled, and only Medal of Honor winners, men killed in action in Vietnam, and high Cabinet officials and their families are allowed the honor of burial in these hallowed grounds. The government began "phasing out" the national cemeteries several years ago, but its "phase-out" plan did not take into account the increased demand for burial room created by the war in Vietnam. Thus far 20,000 Americans have died in that limited war, and the number rises each day. More land is needed for the nation to bury the men who die in its service. More bodies are on the way.

Appendices

Appendices

JUNGLE WAR

Weak sun-rays out of winter cloud;
the dusty windowpane crossed once by a dark bird.
In a far room the baby cries aloud;
between us two, no word.

But heightened by the lonely cry,
tropical silence in us sets its traps and harkens.
Old grudges deepen and intensify,
and outside the sky darkens.

Under the books, the knickknack shelves,
the shreds of cobweb that still hold our lives together,
we penetrate the jungles of ourselves.
Bombs burst, touched by a feather.

Can no one stop this dull, mad war?
Each still avoids the other's unimpassioned kiss.
O, we no longer know what we longed for.
Maybe it was this.

Richard Moore

APPENDIX B: A Dream

I had a dream that I was invited to the White House. I
didn't want to go because I felt it would be an endorsement
of the war, but on the other hand I *did* want to go, just to see
the White House and all. Well, I went, and there was a big
dance going on, and I just hoped the President wouldn't ask
me to dance. But he saw me across the room and he came
right through the crowd and looked right at me and said
"Ah'd like to dance with the purty little girl." Well, you
can't refuse if the President asks you to dance, so I danced
with him, but I said "Mr. President, I just want you to know
that I strongly disapprove of your policy in Vietnam." But
he didn't seem to hear, and he just kept smiling and dancing.
The thing that surprised me was that he was a wonderful
dancer, and I kept wanting to go on dancing with him even
though I didn't really like him and didn't think I even ought
to be there at the White House if I had stuck to my principles. But the music kept playing and I kept on dancing
with the President. The next morning I woke up feeling
awful.

—A dream that was dreamed by
Barbara, a friend, in Washington, D.C.

APPENDIX C: Excerpt of a Letter to the Author from a
              Christian Minister

DAN—I needed your letter right now, for as I walked with
aging tread up our smelly stairways, I knew that our world
has entered the last stages of the insanity which will soon
finish it . . . and only we who are sane know that we are all
mad.